War and Power in the 21st Century

THEMES FOR THE 21ST CENTURY

Titles in this series

Forthcoming

War and Power in the 21st Century

The State, Military Conflict and the International System

PAUL HIRST

Polity

First published in 2001 by Polity Press in association with Blackwell Publishing Ltd.

Reprinted 2003 , 2004

Editorial office:
Polity Press
65 Bridge Street
Cambridge CB2 1UR, UK

Marketing and production:
Blackwell Publishing Ltd
108 Cowley Road
Oxford OX4 1JF, UK

Published in the USA by
Blackwell Publishing Inc.
350 Main Street
Malden, MA 02148, USA

ISBN 0-7456-2520-7
ISBN 0-7456-2521-5 (pbk)

A catalogue record for this book is available from the British Library and has been applied for from the Library of Congress.

Typeset in 10.5 on 12 pt Plantin
by SetSystems Ltd, Saffron Walden, Essex

Printed and bound in Great Britain by
Marston Book Services Limited, Oxford

This book is printed on acid-free paper.

Contents

Acknowledgements

Thanks are due for suggestions and comments to James Hamilton-Patterson, Lars Bo Kaspersen, Tim Megarry, Terry Meyer, Grahame Thompson and Jonathan Zeitlin.

Introduction

It has become commonplace to speculate on the future after the turn of the millennium. In one sense such periods are arbitrary, as are centuries. Yet we are living in a period when the prevailing political and economic structures are widely perceived not merely to be changing but subject to radical transformation. In the case of the sovereign territorial state it has existed for a large part of the past millennium, for four hundred years. Thus speculation may be not merely fashionable but necessary. The aim of this short book is to examine likely developments in state power, armed conflict, and in the nature of the international system in this coming century. It will consider how the various transformational forces such as changes in military technology, developments in communications and information technology, changing economic structures, processes of environmental degradation, and evolving political sources of conflict and cooperation will impact on war, interstate relations, and patterns of national and supranational governance.

So many things are changing that it would be foolish either to project forward current institutions and circumstances, or to construct futuristic scenarios. Both are likely to be wrong. We cannot rely, for example, on projecting forward China's current official growth rate for the next twenty-five years and assuming it will become the largest economy on the planet and a rival to the USA, or on imagining possible future wars between the Great Powers. Thus we will concentrate on the factors likely to drive the international system during the next century. These may well work in contrary directions. Current trends in communications and international trade, for example, have greatly reduced the value of interstate conflict in achieving economic ends. Countries have easy access to foreign markets. Global warming may change the picture dramatically, however. As sea levels rise and climates change, countries may well fight over access to water, agricultural land, and places to settle. This book tries to be neither alarmist nor complacent. It argues that the state will remain a central political institution, but it also argues that by the end of the century it may operate in a physical and social environment very different from today's. Present conflicts in both interpretation and politics centre on the future of economic globalization. Both the advocates of the present international economic system, and its opponents find it very difficult to imagine an economic situation in which it is physical resources that are the key determinants of policy and in which states play a key role in obtaining access to them and distributing them. Climate change could alter the current logics of economics and politics.

The twenty-first century has not been the only century subject to rapid military, political and economic change. Thus in a book that tries to look forward it is necessary to look back at how states and armed forces have coped with change, and also to consider whether some of those responses remain 'wired' into the states system for the foreseeable future. The first two chapters will set the scene by reviewing past patterns in war and international relations. The second two will look forward to the future of armed conflict and the future of the international system.

Chapter 1 considers the transformations in weapons, military organization and forms of warfare from the beginning of the sixteenth century to the present day. It looks at past revolutions in military affairs to provide a standard of measure against which to judge the current claims that we are in a period of revolutionary change. An account of military change that goes back to the 1500s is not excessive in its historical depth in providing a context for modern war, because many of the basic features of modern war and military organization were created in this period (which coincided with the formation of the modern states system) and are still with us.

The second chapter on the formation and development of the modern states system from the sixteenth century onwards has similar objectives. The reasons for returning to this period of the rise of the modern state some 300–400 years ago and concentrating on it for a large part of this chapter are threefold. The first is that certain of the forces active in the constitution of the states system are not merely historical but are still at work in it. Thus there is a strong tendency in the modern international system to reinforce exclusive territorial governance. Supranational agencies of governance, while widespread today, are limited to specific functions and are legitimated and underwritten by territorial states.

The second and related reason is to consider the factors that led the international system to converge on one dominant type of political organization, the modern state. The current period is one of rapid change and volatility in both economics and politics. This leads to exaggerated claims based on rash extrapolations from often short-term trends. One such claim is that the nation-state is in near terminal decline and that there are transformations in the basic structures of social and political organization as radical as those of the sixteenth and seventeenth centuries. Will such

changes lead to a new set of selection pressures – working
in a different direction from those of Renaissance Europe
– that will lead to convergence on a new dominant type of
social organization, such as the transnational company?
There are reasons to be profoundly sceptical about such
claims and looking in detail at a previous period of transformation helps to explain why.

The third reason for looking at the history of the states
system from its formation up to the end of the Cold War
is to demystify beliefs that certain features of the modern
period are unique. The contemporary concern with human
rights in other countries, for example, while distinctive in
content, is not unprecedented. The rights of individuals
and collectivities have been of importance since the consolidation of the states system. Thus confessional rights
were a crucial issue in the seventeenth century, dominated
as it was by religious concerns. The abolition of the slave
trade and the right of nations to self-determination were
key concerns in the international politics of the nineteenth
century. It should also be obvious that what is called
'globalization', that is, an open international economy and
the widespread adoption of economic liberalism as state
policy, is not in fact new, but was fully developed before
1914. The first half of the twentieth century saw the
collapse of this liberal economy and the struggle between
democratic and authoritarian states for primacy and survival. The liberal system was rebuilt on the basis of democratic military victory and it continues in a modified form
today. We should be aware that the international economic
system has been subject to major changes since 1850 and
that an open trading order is not a 'natural' state of affairs
but has social and political foundations.

Chapter 3 considers the future of war. It looks at the
current balance of power between the major states. It
considers the fashionable thesis that the principal conflicts

of the future will be 'new wars' within states and that the role of the major Western powers will be to intervene to preserve human rights. The 'revolution in military affairs' is assessed, with the conclusion that major changes in military technology are in train, driven by several current and emergent technologies. The full impact of such changes is some way off but may lead to major alterations in the balance of power, since it may favour those on the defence and may enable lesser powers to compete with the USA. Lastly, the chapter will examine the possible impact of environmental crisis on future conflicts, and the future of China as a potential rival to the USA.

Chapter 4 considers the future of the state and the international system. It argues that the state is not in decline, having examined the evidence for the forces that are supposed to be undermining it. It pays particular attention to economic globalization and the new communications media. However, having demonstrated that the state and something like the current international system will persist, the argument changes direction and challenges fashionable economic liberal ideas that all economies and companies will converge on American models. Thus the system is likely to become more polycentric and conflictual. Lastly it is argued that the prospects for greater democracy in global governance are poor, since inequalities of wealth and power are too great. That is no reason to do nothing; in the absence of a determined effort to reduce such inequalities and to tackle the consequences of climate change by the major advanced nations, the present institutions of global governance will become ever more illegitimate and thus ineffective.

The theoretical position of this text could best be described as a form of modified realism. Although well aware of the numerous theoretical challenges to realism and neorealism, the author is not deterred by them. It is a central proposition of this book that the form of liberal and open international economy developed since 1945 reinforces the saliency of the state, and gives its status as the principal political actor across national borders a new and enhanced role. The advanced states seek above all to promote the economic interests of their companies and citizens. They underwrite international law and supranational economic governance as part of the process of doing so. They also use force when the basic rules of the international system are challenged. Access to markets means that the advanced states and all lesser states that support the free trading regime do not currently have to use force against each other to pursue their dominant foreign policy concerns, which are currently economic. If this context of economic liberalism changes, then the objectives of states, the constraints on them, and their behaviour will change to something more like that of the more openly conflictual interstate relations of the past.

1

Military Revolutions

It is widely believed that we are in a period of revolutionary change in warfare, called by its proponents the 'revolution in military affairs' (RMA). Military technology, the organization of the armed forces, and the nature and purposes of war are possibly in the process of being rapidly transformed. These changes seem to have come together and to have accelerated with the end of the Cold War. Some of the claims made for the RMA, that it will eliminate the 'fog' of war and that it will cement the permanent dominance of the offensive over the defensive are so sweeping that it is necessary to place them in context. Revolutions in military affairs are neither new nor does the present one seem to be unprecedented in scale, despite the claims of some of its advocates. The modern world has been shaped by two major military revolutions and by two significant changes in military technology that followed rapidly after the second transformative revolution.

The gunpowder revolution of the sixteenth century that coincided with the formation of the modern sovereign territorial state is the first major military revolution. The application of the industrial revolution to war that began in the mid-nineteenth century is the second. This latter revolution led to the total wars that dominated the first half of the twentieth century and that have shaped to a

considerable degree the institutions and the balance of
power in the world we now inhabit. The mechanization of
war and the advent of nuclear weapons followed closely in
the wake of this second great transformation at fifty-year
intervals. The one has defined the current conventional
forces of the major powers, and the other has determined
why such forces cannot be effectively used by such powers
one against the other.

The causes, courses and effects of these two major
revolutions have much to teach us, in particular what
rapid change in military technology does to create pressures for change in armed forces, societies, and interstate
relations. Technological change emerges from a set of
social conditions and social pressures for new technical
adaptations. It is itself caused and is not a pure exogenous
force. But certain changes once set in train seem to act as
if they were just such a force and oblige the ensemble of
social relations around them to adapt to them. Thus
specific technological innovations are closely followed by
major changes in military organization and in the wider
society. Such subsequent organizational and social
changes are by no means simple and direct effects of the
changing means of warfare. They are specific social innovations and are in turn necessary in order to realize the
full power of the new weapons.[1]

This chapter will focus mainly on technological change
in warfare, but as it progresses it will become clear that
such changes often have complex and even contradictory
effects on political structures and international relations.
This should caution us against predicting direct and unme-
diated political and social effects from the current military
changes. The long period of technological stagnation
between 1650 and 1850 should also remind us that technical change is not necessarily continuous. This was a
period in which the defence was dominant and was coun-

teracted chiefly by social and political factors that changed the size, competence or motivation of the armed forces of one of the major powers. It may thus be possible that after a period of rapid and major change in the next half-century military technology will begin to come up against basic limitations of information and engineering technologies. A burst of radical change followed by stasis is thus perfectly possible.

In both the sixteenth and the nineteenth centuries contemporaries were well aware of the changes taking place and sought to understand and master them. The periods 1500–1650 and 1815–1950 both produce a large literature of military commentary and wider reflection on war. Intellectuals and military intellectuals struggled to come to terms with the new changes and to reconfigure them in ways they thought appropriate. The caricature view of a hidebound aristocracy unable to adapt to gunpowder weapons in the first period and a rigid military set in the Napoleonic mode unable to understand the killing power of the new weapons in the second is just too neat. Established elites proved remarkably responsive to change. War is driven by ideas about how to use weapons and military systems almost as much as it is by technical and organizational changes themselves. Ideas are thus crucial and we shall pay considerable attention to current ideas about future wars and future weapons in chapter 3. We shall be lucky to achieve the same levels of understanding and effective response as intellectuals, both military and civilian, did in earlier periods of radical change.

The military revolution of the sixteenth century

The first 'military revolution debate' began with the publi-
cation of Michael Roberts's *The Military Revolution
1560–1660* in 1956 and it has produced a vast and ever-
growing historical literature.[2] This controversy largely
turns on how, where or when the revolution happened.
There were huge changes in war, state and society between
1500 and 1700. Historians squabble about which changes
and which specific subperiod were the most important, or
they pick the whole period and say a revolution happened
because things were vastly different at the end of the whole
period than at the beginning. It would be tiresome to
summarize this historiographical battle in great detail in a
book that tries to anticipate the future, but some attention
to the issues is essential. In particular it helps to challenge
the excessive claims made for the political effects of the
Military Revolution by many social scientists. I shall contend that the initial forces driving change were technological and that their effects were well in train before Roberts's
revolution begins in 1560. Indeed, the changes he
describes can be seen as a subsequent process of adaptation of military tactics and organization to these effects and
to fully exploit the potential of the new weapons.

Something radical did happen at the turn of the fifteenth
and sixteenth centuries. In 1494 the French King Charles
VIII led an army into Italy and in the process transformed
warfare in the peninsula and began a decisive period of
military change up to 1559. During this time France and
the Spanish-Habsburg Empire fought for supremacy. Central to the early French success was a large siege train of
modern highly mobile bronze cannon firing iron shot.

These guns rapidly demolished the fragile and often ill-maintained walls of the Italian cities and fortresses. This unlocked the positional warfare that had brought stasis to war in Italy for the better part of a century. Within a year the French had traversed the peninsula and entered Naples, an unprecedented feat. Contemporaries were well aware of this. The historian and politician Francesco Guicciardini rightly saw the French invasion as both a revolutionary form of war and a fundamental transformation of Italian politics.[3]

Guns, of course, were not new in 1494. They had been in use since the fourteenth century and had grown dramatically in effectiveness since the mid-fifteenth. In 1453 the Turks used cannon to breach the walls of Constantinople. In the same year the new artillery created by the Bureau brothers completed the destruction of the English position in France. This had depended on a network of castles and fortified towns laboriously acquired in the course of the Hundred Years' War. The castle and the fortified town had evolved to the point where relatively small garrisons could hold out against a large besieging force. This gave the defending state the time to mobilize a field army to threaten the besiegers and thus relieve the place. The rapid fall of place after place in the face of the new artillery overwhelmed the capacity of the English to respond with the limited field forces available to them. Warfare shifted from the dominance of the defence to that of the offensive.

What was new in 1494 was the further advanced mobility and hitting power of cannon, but what was revolutionary was the response to them. The scale of the shock in the Italian city-states set off a rapid adaptational response in fortification. Italian fortifications had been changing in response to gunpowder since the 1470s and Italian architects were the most advanced in producing new ideas. The early sixteenth century was a period of experimentation and sustained innovation. By the 1530s the first complete examples of the new system of fortification were built and would become the accepted standard solution to artillery for the next three hundred years. This was based on curtain walls that were covered against artillery fire by being sunk behind ditches and screened by an earth *glacis*. The walls had arrowhead bastions at their corners, each capable of supporting the others nearest to it with inter-locking fields of fire. Contemporaries were sufficiently aware of the source of the innovation that they called the new layout of arrowhead bastions the *trace italienne*.

What the new system of fortification did was to restore the balance between defence and offence, and then shift it back strongly in favour of the former as the century progressed. By the 1580s, wherever the new fortifications were widely adopted, warfare became a positional struggle, once again dominated by sieges. Thus the Eighty Years' War, which secured the independence of the Netherlands from Spain, was essentially an attempt by the Spaniards to break through the dense fortified belt of Dutch towns. The new siege warfare was expensive both in manpower and money. It helped to make warfare protracted and indeci-sive, with armies slowly marching and countermarching within the fortified zones or tied down in major sieges.

This indecisiveness of war had one major political effect; it helped to prevent the formation of an imperial hegemony in Europe. Fortifications were central in checking the Habsburg bid for mastery in Europe and also in containing the Ottoman attempt to break into Central Europe and into the Western Mediterranean. The Habsburg Empire failed to overcome the Protestant powers in Germany, and Spain failed in the Netherlands. The Ottomans were checked at two major sieges, Vienna in 1529 and Malta in 1565. Spain and the Ottomans could not fully exploit the advantages in manpower and fiscal resources that followed from their extensive empires and turn them into a stable hegemony over other states. This ensured the survival of a population of roughly equal competing territorial states. The states system that formed coherently in the second half of the seventeenth century and that characterized Europe until the First World War thus owed a considerable amount to the underlying indecisiveness of warfare brought about in large measure by this first part of the gunpowder revolution. Lest this be thought to overstate the case, bear in mind that Spain and the Turks had numerical superiority over lesser states and were the most effective military powers of their day.[4] Had warfare favoured the offensive, the outcome could well have been two imperial hegemonies, one Catholic and one Muslim, confronting one another.

The success of France in Italy was short-lived. In 1495 the Spaniards landed in Italy to check the French. At Cerignola in 1503 the Spanish inflicted a serious defeat on the French. They did so by using entrenched infantry armed with firearms. In a series of engagements up to Ceresole in 1544 the arquebus (an early musket) and field artillery transformed tactics. Gunpowder weapons made the defence decisive in the field as well as in the new fortifications. Combat tactics now turned around achieving a strategically advantageous position and fighting from behind prepared defences if possible. Heavy cavalry became more and more ineffective as the century proceeded. Pikes (long spears), from being a decisive weapon of war in the fifteenth century in the hands of the Swiss, became increasingly a cover for the growing numbers of arquebusiers in armies.

A minimally competent arquebusier could be produced with about six weeks basic training. Printing made simple basic training manuals available throughout Europe. They broke down into a series of simple and easily repeated steps the actions of loading and firing a musket and handling a pike.[5] The result was that small *cadres* of experienced soldiers and enthusiastic amateurs could quickly train large improvised armies. Such manuals helped to train the rapidly assembled armies of the English Civil War. Gunpowder weapons made soldiers easy to recruit and replace. This reduced their status. The new systems of training represented a kind of early-modern Taylorism and deskilling. The new weapons also made soldiers cheaper. This, combined with the large numbers of poor and unemployed produced by the economic changes and the price revolution of the sixteenth century, made it possible to raise larger armies. It also meant that it was possible to replace armies after a major defeat and to create rebel armies to defy hated rulers.

It is widely held that military changes in the sixteenth century increased the cost of war and thus favoured the centralization of power and the rise of the modern state. The central state was able to eliminate all lesser powers and establish a monopoly of the means of violence. This might hold true in relation to the lesser nobility, who could stretch to a few armed retainers and a run-down castle, but they had not been in the business of challenging monarchs for some time. Major wealthy cities and lesser powers had the chance with the new weapons to defy centralization or annexation. Thus the Grand Duchy of Mantua used the modern fortifications to preserve its independence during the Italian wars.[6] The armies of the religious wars in France and Germany, of the Dutch rebellion, the English Civil War, and the various localist revolts of the mid-seventeenth century were raised in defiance of established authority and many of these challenges succeeded. The modern sovereign territorial state was formed in a century and a half of religious, localist and social struggles in which the large centralizing powers were not always victorious. Spain was defeated in the Netherlands, so was the Imperialist cause in Germany, and so was the Stuart monarchy in England.

Gunpowder did not destroy the feudal order. Its economic and political foundations were in advanced dissolution by 1500 in Western Europe. The nobilities of Europe reinvented themselves as commercial landowners or as state servants. The new states competing against one another and struggling with internal religious conflicts and localist revolts were administratively fragile and often unable to impose anything resembling a monopoly of the means of violence. All the major states faced repeated crises of authority in the sixteenth and early seventeenth centuries. Religious conflicts divided society ideologically. Catholics and Protestants fought for dominance within states, tearing the political fabric apart, and states aided religious rebels in other countries for either ideological affinity or reason of state. The Reformation sparked off a European civil war far more extended and savage than that between Communists and Fascists in the 1930s.

However, by the mid-seventeenth century most states had mastered internal armed conflicts and had begun to control religious dissent. The French state defeated the Huguenots militarily in 1628 and had managed to overcome a series of noble and localist revolts called the Fronde by 1653. Spain defeated the revolt of the Catalans, but was unable to prevent the reassertion of Portuguese independence. England achieved a measure of political stability by restoring Charles II in 1660. The effect of the Peace of Westphalia in 1648 that ended the Thirty Years' War was to stabilize the relationship between religion and territory in Germany. Germany was the key centre of the religious wars and the 'black hole' that undermined what forms of stability there were in the emerging international system by sucking in external powers to interfere on behalf of their co-religionists. The treaty recognized that certain states were henceforth Catholic or Protestant, accepting the balance of power as it stood, and it represented the defeat of the aim of the Imperial party to assert Catholic hegemony. The external powers that had intervened in Germany, France and Sweden, in particular, agreed to abide by the religious truce in Germany and not to interfere in the internal affairs of the member states of the Empire.

Westphalia initiates the widespread acceptance of the principle of non-interference. That principle and the corresponding obligation of mutual recognition are what make states sovereign. Each state is accepted as a legitimate member of the system without reference to ideology. Given non-interference in its internal religious affairs by other states, the state can effectively use its administrative and military capacities against internal enemies. Thus the international dimension of mutual recognition is central to the state's acquisition of a monopoly of the means of violence within its territory. Non-interference and mutual recognition require that the political entities conform to the model of the sovereign state, each of which is the exclusive controller of a definite territory.

The reason for raising these international system issues here, returning to them in chapter 2, is that they are central in explaining both the periodicity of the major states' acquisition of the capacity for external violence – why there is a dramatic change around 1660 – and the nature of the wars fought, with the shift from complex wars with mixed motives, including intervention to aid religious compatriots, to wars based on interstate rivalries. Agreements between states were crucial in fostering their capacity to control their own societies. Once they had done so they could systematize their means of violence and direct it outwards.

It would be ludicrous to derive all these changes from the gunpowder revolution. But fortresses and muskets did play a crucial role in creating the balance of power that was formally recognized in 1648. Writing in the latter part of the eighteenth century Edward Gibbon contended that gunpowder weapons had made civilized peoples secure against barbarians, thus avoiding the fate that befell the Roman Empire.[7] Certainly gunpowder weapons vastly increased the power of European states against non-European peoples, but if anything one could turn Gibbon on his head. Gunpowder made Europe safe against anything resembling the Roman Empire, that is, the hegemony of one state.

The new gunpowder weapons were at first inserted into late medieval armies. These were mostly mercenary forces, augmented with a component of nobles and retainers serving under feudal obligations. By the end of the sixteenth century modern military organizations had begun to emerge. The most advanced were the Spanish, followed by the Dutch. The combination of pike and shot encouraged the formation of relatively small units that could coordinate fire and protection (although large pike squares continued to be formed). Such units created an articulated army capable of being deployed by strategic direction. In the sixteenth century interest in Roman military writings was widespread. The Roman legions had been the last great European army capable of being deployed tactically in organized multiple units: cohorts and centuries. In the sixteenth century most of the modern military ranks (general, colonel, captain and lieutenant) emerged.

However, most armies until well into the seventeenth century were tactically and administratively ramshackle. They were raised by states that were still fiscally fragile and could not bear the costs of large standing armies, let alone administer them efficiently. Most soldiers were mercenaries engaged for a campaign by private military contractors acting on an official commission. Standing armies of disciplined troops were a creation of the later seventeenth century and most soldiers were not housed in barracks and subject to twenty-four-hour supervision until the late eighteenth century, if then. The widespread adoption of the bayonet in the 1690s enabled every soldier to become a musketeer, greatly increasing the firepower of armies. This put a strong emphasis on linear formations to maximize fire effect and, therefore, an even greater emphasis on drill in order to keep such extended lines level. This improved the firepower effectiveness of armies greatly but was not equivalent in scope to the revolution brought about by gunpowder weapons in the early 1500s.

The revolution in weapons was not paralleled by any corresponding change in the conditions of warfare. War was limited by certain fundamental constraints. First, low agricultural productivity. This limited the number of men who could be sustainably taken from civilian life into the army in normal times and, even in times of economic dislocation when there was a large surplus labour supply, restricted recruits mainly to paupers, criminals and vagabonds. More significantly, it limited the ability of armies to live off the land, even in well-developed regions like Flanders. Second, bad roads limited mobility, especially in wet weather. These two factors together meant that it was difficult to assemble more than about 30,000 men in any one region and hope to feed them successfully. Third, armies found it difficult to keep the field in winter, when food was scarce and cold and damp increased susceptibility to disease. Armies typically campaigned in the summer season and hoped to capture one or two fortified positions where they might winter. If they failed they had typically to retreat and disperse.

Weak state administrations, fiscal fragility, physical constraints on operations, and the bias toward the defensive made decisive campaigns difficult to sustain. Large armies could be assembled, like the 134,000 men nominally under the Imperialist command of General Wallenstein at the start of the campaigning season in 1629. But they usually soon diminished due to desertion and disease. Only a small fraction of such armies could be assembled in the field to any strategic purpose. War tended to break down into dispersed operations and sieges. At worst it became a broken-backed form of conflict in which rival bands of soldiers raided and plundered in a manner indistinguishable from banditry. The civilian population then suffered greatly as rival armies tried to live off the other's territory. The Thirty Years' War degenerated into just such a stalemate, for all the great and supposedly 'decisive' battles, like the Swedish victory over the Imperialists at Breitenfeld in 1631.

These limiting conditions were not relaxed until well into the eighteenth century. The first to be relaxed was the fiscal. The Netherlands and then England created the institutional conditions for the deficit financing of wars at low rates of interest. Investors could be certain that the Bank of England would repay its debts. Lending to the Bank became a secure investment and attracted *rentiers* and not just short-term major speculators. Britain thus enjoyed a decisive fiscal advantage in its wars with France and Spain in the eighteenth century: it could borrow more for less. Second, states began to create effective administrative machines with professional salaried staffs that enabled them to run standing armies and navies. Third, agricultural productivity increased slowly and steadily in the eighteenth century and population grew rather faster. Lastly, roads improved significantly in the eighteenth century both in the density of the network and the quality of the surfaces, at least in the most developed parts of Europe. Where a dearth of roads hindered military mobility and state control, as in Scotland after the 1745 rebellion, military roads were built between strategic points.

Warfare was almost continuous in the eighteenth century. The major states strove for advantage in the struggles to preserve the balance of power, to gain territory, and to keep or capture profitable colonies overseas. The Seven Years' War of 1756–63 was fought in Europe but also in North America, the Caribbean and India. Yet warfare remained constrained by the fact that most states in the international system were dynastic. What transformed the limits on the scale and sustainability of operations was not a new technology, but a gradual lifting of the physical constraints throughout the century and a political revolution at its end.

Changes in war have regularly been anticipated by military intellectuals. Thus the French military reformer Jacques Comte de Guibert contended in 1772:

> Only suppose the appearance in Europe of a people who should join to the austere virtues and a citizen army a fixed plan of aggression, who should stick to it, who – understanding how to conduct war economically and to live at enemy expense – should not be driven to give up by financial exhaustion. Such a people would subdue its neighbours and overthrow our feeble constitutions like the gale aquilon bends the reeds.[8]

This is exactly what happened after 1793, when the French revolutionary armies were loosed upon Europe. Key to the transformation of war made possible by the Revolution and systematized under Napoleon was the change in political goals. Dynastic states had fought for limited political advantages, typically to realize an inheritance of territory or prevent another state from benefiting from one. States oriented to external commerce fought to seize opportunities for trade and colonies. Napoleon sought hegemony for France in Europe in a way far beyond even the ambitions of Louis XIV. He sought to subordinate or destroy enemy regimes by destroying their capacity to fight, defeating their armies in major battles. French strategy relied on the inability of ancien régime states to call forth an equivalent national resistance. Second, the Revolution made possible conscription, the *levée en masse*, greatly increasing the number of available troops. Conscription pushed military participation up to the limit of social sustainability. Ancien régime states typically paid mercenaries to fight, they faced severe fiscal constraints, and they had a limited religious and dynastic bond between rulers and ruled. Having less legitimacy and less coercive power than the Revolutionary regime, they could not draw as deeply on the lives and property of their peoples.

Napoleon used the new mass armies to side-step the network of fortresses. Aiming ultimately at the enemy's capital, he sought to destroy their main field army. The French advanced on a broad front, in several dispersed columns, each of about 30,000 men. This strategy used the road network and food supplies to a maximum. Each column had sufficient power to defend if attacked. The aim was that they would converge on a strategic point and overwhelm the enemy, as Napoleon did in 1805 at Ulm and 1806 at Jena.

Napoleonic warfare encountered three fundamental obstacles that ensured that the French bid for hegemony in Europe failed. First, in Spain and Russia the French campaigned in countries where the old limitations on warfare reasserted themselves: poor roads and low agricultural productivity. These countries were not merely materially backward, they were also socially far enough behind that the population was immune to the revolutionary message. Spanish traditional elites and the peasantry alike rallied in defence of the old social order against Enlightenment modernization imposed from Madrid. Russian serfs likewise rallied to Tsar and Church. Second, in Germany the French victories set off a nationalist response that gave Prussia a spurt of reform that renewed social and military institutions. It was reinforced by a popular pan-German revival against the French, rallying pusillanimous conservative elites to the people rather than the other way round. Thirdly, the chief commercial power, Britain, was beyond the reach of French armies and was able to subsidize the continental powers. With the end of the Napoleonic bid for European hegemony, 1815 restored not merely the traditional rulers but also a world of medium-sized territorial states governed by balance of power considerations.

The period after 1815 produced what is still the most profound reflection on war, Carl von Clausewitz's *On War*.[9] Clausewitz combined the experience of the Napoleonic system of warfare with the world of states restored by the peace of Vienna. Clausewitz's large work can be summarized in some key propositions. War is in essence a combat, reciprocal action between two opponents. To win one must anticipate, match, and overwhelm one's opponent. War tends to escalate to extremes (to what Clausewitz called absolute war) but all actual operations are threatened by the unanticipated difficulties and obstacles that Clausewitz called 'friction'. Reciprocal action and friction mean that military operations cannot be planned bureaucratically; they require imagination, initiative, morale and willpower. War thus demands talents and virtues on the part of soldiers, and superior morale and will-to-win can be decisive. War principally involves disciplined military forces. The true aim of operations should be to destroy the enemy's capacity to fight. This involves seeking decisive engagements. War takes place between states. It is, as Clausewitz says, 'the continuation of policy by other means'. Soldiers are thus servants of the state; they try to realize the ends of their political masters but in a specific medium with its own logic. Equally, policy-makers have to accept the distinctiveness of military affairs and let soldiers win wars in the only way they can. The defensive is the strongest form of war and it can only be overcome with superior numbers and a willingness by soldiers to sacrifice their lives. Modern war thus implies mass armies and the creation of forms of legitimacy that will tie soldiers to the regime.

Clausewitz defined a military doctrine for a world of competing states, each of which followed a foreign policy dictated by reason of state, but in which, if they were to be militarily effective, there were forms of inclusive political order that tied soldiers to their state. These features of Clausewitzian war held good well into the twentieth century. Nationalism tied mass armies to the state and offered a wider focus of loyalty than the old dynastic regimes, even if the nation-states were still monarchies. War did remain the continuation of policy. All states were following classical reason of state considerations in 1914. They got into a war that could only be ended by brutal attrition, but in which the Clausewitzian emphasis on morale and staying power proved decisive. Even Hitler's war could, at the outset in 1939, be presented as an attempt to recover Germany's losses in the First World War and to renew its bid to be the dominant power in Europe. Clausewitz's division of labour between soldiers and politicians survived in a new form adapted to the necessities of total war. The industrialization of war inevitably brought politicians into military strategy, and military objectives had to be conditioned by economic constraints. Equally the militarization of industry forced generals to become politicians and managers. Where politicians crossed the line and began continually to direct operations, as Hitler did after 1941, the results were disastrous. Equally, where the military gained control over political ends and the civilian economy, as Hindenburg and Ludendorff did after 1916, the results were mostly dire too. The modern commander as manager (mediating between generals and politicians and balancing the conflicting demands on grand strategy) is exemplified by Eisenhower in 1944–45.

War in the industrial age 1850–1918

The innovations of the sixteenth-century gunpowder revolution were finite. Once they were accomplished the pace of technical change slowed down; there was no process of continuous revolutionary technical innovation. The same could largely be said about innovations in military organization after the formation of standing armies and the administrative and fiscal infrastructure necessary to support them in the later seventeenth century. The major transformation in military organization, mass conscription, was not universally adopted and did not become general until the latter half of the nineteenth century. England and Russia did not adopt it and the French themselves dropped it after 1815 and did not revert to it again until after 1870. Between 1550 and 1850 military technology underwent gradual and incremental evolutionary change. It was much more effective towards the end of the period, but the basic weapons were essentially the same. To illustrate the point, a sailor from the English ships of the Armada campaign in 1588 would have been quickly at home in the ships that fought at the battle of Trafalgar in 1805. Likewise, a soldier from the sieges of the Italian wars of the sixteenth century would have understood exactly what was happening at the siege of Badajoz in Wellington's Peninsular campaign in 1812. The musket of the Napoleonic Wars differed little from that of the late seventeenth century and achieved only modest increases in hitting power and range over the arquebus. Muzzle-loading cannon in 1800 were more effective than in 1600 but their range and the practical upper limits of weight of shot were about the same. Warships were propelled by sails and fought with broadside-mounted cannon. Bastioned trace fortresses were still being built in the early nineteenth century.

From 1850 onwards, however, the industrial revolution rapidly and continuously transformed war. The *Dreadnought* of 1905 would have been all but incomprehensible to a sailor from the *Victory* of 1805. For example, it had a practical maximum range some twenty times greater and projectiles some twenty-five times heavier. A soldier from the English trenches before Sebastopol in the Crimean War of 1854 would have found the German destruction of the Belgian ring of concrete forts around Liège in 1914 equally beyond comprehension. The siege guns of 1854 could fire shells of 30kg some 400 metres maximum effective range to batter walls. Krupp howitzers could fire shells weighing 1 tonne some 6,000 metres to destroy several metres of reinforced concrete. War changed utterly in its basic technologies in the thirty years between 1850 and 1880. Weapons were typically obsolete before they had entered service. Military leaders and military intellectuals struggled to adapt. For all the castigation of aristocratic military conservatism by modern scholars it is a miracle that they managed to do so at all. Again, as in the early sixteenth century, the changes were driven by new technologies. What was different this time was that technical change was not confined to weapons – in fact the main forces transforming war were production and communication technologies – and also that technical change was continuous and cumulative.

In the first half of the nineteenth century a cluster of innovations revolutionized the physical conditions of war: canning, railways, steamships and telegraphs. Canning enabled armies to store food better and to supplement biscuit with protein. This enabled them to assemble food in advance and lessened their dependence on local food supplies. Armies could now fight in areas devoid of local food supplies, as in the Crimea or the Wilderness Campaign in the American Civil War. Adequately fed armies could survive winter campaigning too. Railways trebled the speed of movement and vastly increased carrying capacity; they also greatly extended the distance over which troops could be moved and supplied. This made possible the mobilization of mass armies and their delivery to the frontier in a short time. Once they left the railhead, armies returned to the old conditions of movement, limited by the pace of walking with heavy kit and the speed of the horse-drawn supply wagon. The German attack on France in 1914 involved swift mobilization by rail up to the Belgian border. Thereafter, the army had to walk. It failed to meet its targets, falling behind the timetable in the Schlieffen Plan and short of Paris. This enabled the French to mount a last-minute counterattack.

Railways transformed war *within* continents. They had the effect of greatly reducing the advantage that had hitherto prevailed in favour of seaborne as against landborne trade. The result was to make the interiors of continents like the USA or Russia fully exploitable. This was to increase the relative economic strength of land-based powers as against seaborne empires. However, this is not to deny the importance of the revolution in maritime transport that took place in the second half of the nineteenth century. Steamships transformed both maritime commerce and intercontinental warfare. Previously, for example, it had normally taken up to six months to reach India with sailing ships, and arrival was uncertain, since ships could find themselves becalmed. Once coaling stations were in place the journey could be done in as many weeks and reliably. Intercontinental warfare had existed in the sailing ship era. What steam did was to make it possible to transport and supply mass armies overseas. Without it the world wars of the twentieth century would have been impossible. In particular, American armies could not have been supported across the Atlantic and Pacific. The armies that operated outside Europe in the sailing ship era were small. The forces that fought in the North American interior in the eighteenth century were tiny. In India the European powers created armies out of local sepoys and expanded their control by intervening in local conflicts. Their armies were fed and paid for within the subcontinent.

Without the telegraph, railways were only of limited use. Telegraphs coordinated movements and integrated the separate lines into a network. They also made the control of army movements possible, as close as cable could be laid to the front. Once the intercontinental telegraph cables were laid across the Atlantic and to Asia from the 1870s, European powers could control the movements of fleets and armies across the world. The telegraph made possible strategic, and thus political, direction and greatly reduced the scope of local military control. By 1914 local commanders could also bombard their front-line troops with instructions by field telephone. The telegraph set up the conflict between central strategic direction and local front-line knowledge that has persisted to this day, and which the modern Revolution in Military Affairs is supposed to dissolve. The adoption of radio in the years immediately preceding 1914 further increased the capacity to control from above, particularly in allowing commanders to communicate with ships at sea.

One more thing was needed totally to transform war, new forms of firepower. This came in the 1850s with the widespread adoption of the Minié rifle. This was still a muzzle-loader, but one capable of firing accurately out to 1,000 metres. This transformed combat. Even with a slow firing weapon the effective killing zone increased from about 100 metres to 500 metres. The effects were clear in the American Civil War. The Confederate charges at Gettysburg in 1863 were classic examples of Napoleonic élan; their complete destruction showed just how much the already considerable power of the defensive had been reinforced. The mass armies of the Union were armed with Minié rifles. The new lethality was combined with mass production.

Since the War of 1812 between the USA and Britain American military administrators had been seeking standardized and interchangeable weapon parts. The initial reasons were a concern with uniformity and ease of repair. Standardization was achieved by division of labour, specialized machine tools and precise measuring instruments. These innovations made mass production possible. Three decades of experiment by American officers, a long process of trial and error at government arsenals, created a system of industrial efficiency that was then quickly applied by Colt to revolvers, Singer to sewing machines, and McCormick to agricultural machinery. This American system of manufactures, as it was called in Britain in the nineteenth century, was the basis of the mass armies and industrialized killing of the twentieth.

The coincidence of new technologies facilitating mobility, the widespread adoption of mass conscription, and mass-produced weapons of long-distance lethality created a deadly combination. It ensured that the defensive would be by far the stronger form of warfare and that masses of men would be fed into prolonged battles of attrition in an attempt to overcome it. This was not immediately apparent in the period 1850–1900, not because military leaders were unaware of the effect of the new weapons, but because wars were of short duration, like the Franco-Prussian War of 1870–1. All minimally rational officers realized that the problem was how to cover several hundred metres through a hail of bullets. In an encounter battle the outcome would be decided by the side that prevailed in the initial firefight. Against dug-in infantry the only option was to take heavy casualties. The Russo-Japanese War of 1904–5 seemed to confirm this lesson, but also the possibility of achieving a result. The Japanese had suffered massive losses in storming the fortress of Port Arthur, some 20,000 men killed, but they had shown superior will and had prevailed. The intense but short blood sacrifice seemed justified by the strategic importance of the place. Military intellectuals in the period before 1914 sought to assimilate such lessons from combat and to find ways to make the offensive possible. In the case of the Germans it was to use the tactical defensive in a scheme of strategic advance based upon swift mobilization. In the case of the French it was reliance on relentless human wave attacks sustained by high morale.

Between 1850 and 1880 firepower was transformed far beyond the Minié rifle. Rapid-firing breech-loading rifles increased the rate of fire about ten times. From the 1860s a series of machine guns was introduced, the most effective being the Maxim of 1885 that was fully automatic and capable of firing several hundred times a minute. Field artillery was also transformed by 1900. It increased greatly in range (from about 1,000 to 6,000 metres), in rate of fire (from 1 to up to 15 times per minute) and in the lethality of shells with new high explosives.

What these changes ensured was that, after a short

period of encounter battles, warfare between evenly
matched forces with a reasonable ratio of force to space
would turn into a linear siege. The tendency, started at
Cerignola four hundred years before, was to entrench and
defend, thus exploiting the firepower of the new weapons.
The mass production of barbed wire made such temporary
fortifications all but impregnable. This outcome, which
produced the attrition war of 1914–18, was anticipated by
some intellectuals well before 1914. Many pacifists
believed war had become too costly to sustain. Prolonged
war would wreck complex interdependent systems of trade
and finance. This was a common proposition adopted by
antiwar liberals like Norman Angell and Marxists like
Rudolf Hilferding. Ivan S. Bloch, a Polish banker living in
Paris and writing in 1897, made it plain that a major war
could now only be an extended bloody struggle that would
destroy existing civilization. Bloch claimed: 'Everybody
will be entrenched in the next war. The spade will be as
indispensable to a soldier as his rifle. . . . All wars will of
necessity partake of the character of siege operations . . .
soldiers may fight as they please; the ultimate decision is in
the hand of famine.'[10]

Bloch was prescient. Hunger did play a major part in
deciding the First World War. Both sides tried to starve
one another out, the Allies with blockade and the Germans
with submarines. The Germans seemed to have starved
themselves, food shortages figuring prominently in the
collapse of morale among civilians and the consequent
revolt of the Fleet in 1918. But Bloch and other liberal
commentators were wrong about the inevitability of economic collapse. Commercial civilization *was* fragile. Industrial societies were far more robust. The economic losers
in 1914–18 were Britain and France. They had built up
their position of commercial strength throughout the nineteenth century and had become *rentier* nations, having

accumulated large stocks of foreign investments. Britain and France were by far and away the major creditor nations in 1913, with stocks of overseas investments of $18 billion and $9 billion respectively.[11] By 1913 Britain's share of world trade had fallen to 15 per cent but it remained the world's financial and commercial hub.[12] The UK had by far the largest merchant fleet in 1914. It was the centre of the world's markets for commercial bills and insurance. Britain was the lynchpin of the world monetary system based on the Gold Standard. All these assets were exceedingly prone to disruption by war, and the world economy was almost as integrated as it is today.

In 1918 the USA emerged as the main creditor nation, having been the principal debtor in 1913. Britain and France had incurred some $3.7 billion and $2 billion respectively of inter-government debt to the USA.[13] Britain lost 25 per cent and France 50 per cent of their prewar foreign investments.[14] This was crucial for Britain, since income from investments and other invisibles had offset its balance of trade gap before 1914. Britain lost major foreign markets to non-European competitors during the war (more than half its trade was outside Europe and North America in 1913).

If Britain and France were the main losers from the disruption of commercial civilization, the United States was the clear economic beneficiary of the war. This basic change in the balance of economic power has lasted until the present day. During the war all the major combatants harnessed industrial production to the needs of war, adopting whatever financial and fiscal expedients were necessary to supply the fronts. Industry was converted wholesale to military production. Britain and France benefited from being able to draw on the immense productive capacity and food output of North America. Germany was barred from such a source by blockade and its limited access to foreign credit, and forced to utilize its own resources. In all three countries the state took over the management of the economy and the direction of industrial production. Industrial employers, organized labour, and the government cooperated to find means of maximizing output, such as relaxing labour regulations and rationing raw materials. Germany effectively mobilized industrial production but it failed to ensure an adequate supply of food to the civilian population in the later years of the war. It allowed the big agrarian landowners to make excessive profits and the army to requisition excessive amounts of food and horses. Germany failed effectively to exploit its control of a large part of the grain production of Eastern Europe during 1917–18. Britain survived its own food crisis because its system of rationing was fairer and because it was finally able to master the U-boat blockade in 1917–18 by adopting the convoy system for merchant ships.

The economic effects of prolonged war brought about by the new weapons of the late nineteenth century contributed considerably to the economic instability of the period 1919–39, which itself contributed to the renewal of war in 1939–41. The liberal economists of the prewar era were right in that it proved prolonged war had indeed destroyed the open international economy of the *belle époque*. Despite a widespread return to the Gold Standard in the 1920s, it proved impossible to put the old economy back together again. Inflation throughout Europe during the war made it difficult to sustain the old pre-1914 parities to the dollar. The USA failed to sustain the fragile debtor economies of Central Europe. With the Great Crash of 1929 economies across the world went down in the wake of the USA. Britain went off the Gold Standard in 1931 and abandoned free trade for protectionism. The 1930s turned into a struggle between rival protectionist trade blocs for access to raw materials and markets.

Mechanized war 1918–1945

During the First World War the airplane and the tank were introduced as combat weapons. After the war visionary military intellectuals such as J. F. C. Fuller and Guilio Douhet saw them as a way of breaking the deadlock created by firepower and mass production. Fuller initially saw tanks as a kind of land navy, overcoming the obstacles of the front and manoeuvring freely in the enemy's rear. Tanks would render the opponent's armies ineffective and strike at command centres and supply lines. Douhet foresaw aircraft overflying the deadlocked front lines, bombing civilian centres in the rear and reducing the population to terror. Civilian panic would bring down governments and thus end wars. Bombing was like a fast-acting version of blockade.[15]

In fact Fuller and Douhet were too visionary since neither of these technologies was fully mature before the 1940s and neither ever worked as the prophets thought they would. Both technologies had evolved with astounding rapidity since the introduction of the internal combustion engine in the 1890s, but that was part of the problem. In the case of land vehicles civilian automobile industries did not develop fast enough to enable the mass production necessary for fully mechanized war. In the case of the airplane its effectiveness depended on other, unrelated technologies that would enable it to find and hit its targets, and these were still in development in the 1930s.

Tanks were not in fact like landships. They were not an independent weapon but part of a whole military system that included infantry, artillery and supply services. The German *Blitzkrieg* victory in France in 1940 would seem to gainsay this. However, the success of the Panzers was possible because of a mixture of faulty Allied strategy, poor French morale, and cumbersome command structures. It should be remembered that the French had as many tanks as the Germans, but failed to use them effectively. Massive tank assaults could be contained, as the Russians proved at Kursk in 1943. In 1940 the only country with a civilian motor industry large enough to be capable of producing the vehicles for a wholly motorized mass army was the USA. The German army that invaded Russia in 1941 relied on railways for its strategic mobility and on horses for the tactical mobility of about 80 per cent of its forces. Even the American forces in France were hard put to sustain their advance to the German border in 1944. Given the speed of their advance and the destruction of the rail network, they were dependent on fuel carried on trucks to support their armoured spearheads. This supply chain proved inadequate, even when vast numbers of vehicles were diverted to the purpose.

Tanks and planes depended on radio for their coordination. Without it they would be merely of isolated and local use. In the 1930s the invention of radar shifted the balance between defence and offence in the air in favour of the former. Radar-controlled fighters by day forced British and German bombers to operate at night. They found it difficult to find and hit targets as big as major cities. They caused damage but failed to halt war economies, and, contra Douhet, they failed to damage civilian morale – if anything they raised it. Only in 1944–5 did Anglo-American air power prove effective. By then American fighters had begun to control the air by day. Radar navigation and bomb aiming made British mass bomber raids on cities effective. The targeted destruction of the German railways and oil industry wrecked the German war economy far more effectively than the bombing of manufacturing plants themselves. Against weak Japanese air defences mass American fire-bombing raids destroyed entire urban centres. Indeed, Hiroshima and Nagasaki were selected as targets for the atomic bomb because they were among the few Japanese cities of any size that were not completely burnt out.

Given the right conditions, air superiority could thus prove decisive. It could cripple the movement of armies by day and it could damage the war economy. America and its allies have relied on control of the air as their key asset, along with a near monopoly of naval power that enables them to move around the world, ever since. Allied armies were able to compensate for their relative weakness against the Germans by means of air power. They sought to do the same when confronted with the Soviets, seeking to counter numerical superiority with better weapons.

The conventional armed forces of the Cold War were shaped by the experience of the final phase of the conflict in Europe. They brought mechanization to full technological maturity. The platforms that have dominated modern war such as the Abrams tank or the F15 fighter are essentially highly evolved versions of late 1940s technologies. The aviation and motor industries became the core of military mass production after 1945, and tanks and jet planes were turned out in the thousands until the costs of technical evolution cut down production runs from the 1960s onwards. The massive mechanized armed forces of the Cold War were never used in all-out combat in Europe. From being core war-winning weapons, they turned into a form of reinsurance that deterrence would not fail. They prevented conventional thrusts under the nuclear umbrella, establishing a trip-wire and indicating resolve. The forces that fought the Gulf War and that enforced the peace in Bosnia were designed for an impossible all-out battle in central Europe. As we shall see in chapter 3, they may not be the best adapted for future wars.

The advent of nuclear strategy

Nuclear weapons made a fundamental difference to the nature of war because they undermined its rationality. Heretofore, war was a means to an end. It could be highly profitable, as were most of Britain's wars in the eighteenth century or the USA's participation in the two world wars in the twentieth. Nuclear weapons made the rapid escalation to absolute war likely, that is, a generalized exchange in which both the states and societies of the contending powers were destroyed. Nuclear weapons removed the constraints that had limited the destructiveness of war. But, far from reinforcing the offensive, these weapons led to military stalemate. These weapons undermined any possible political objective that their use could serve. The object of nuclear strategy became the paradoxical aim of using the threat of force to avoid war. If nuclear weapons were used, then political strategy had failed. In this case the political effects of this innovation in military technology were fairly direct.

This was recognized immediately after Hiroshima. Bernard Brodie, as prescient as Guibert or Bloch, saw that nuclear weapons had changed the fundamental principles of war between states armed with them: 'Thus far the chief purpose of a military establishment has been to win wars. From now on its chief purpose must be to avert them. It can have no other useful purpose.'[16] Deterrence would give time to work out a political accommodation on the part of the nuclear powers, but it could be no more than that, certainly not a stable condition. Generals were slow to understand this fact that war had changed its nature. Both American and Russian nuclear forces were seen by their militaries into the early 1960s simply as very powerful weapons that in principle could be used. The USA and the USSR did not share a common doctrine of deterrence, but it became clear to politicians that nuclear war would mean the end of civilization. Certainly after the Cuban missile crisis they became profoundly cautious and avoided not merely nuclear threats but situations that could lead to direct military confrontation at the core of the two blocs of states. Deterrence extended beyond nuclear war to other forms of war. War became impossible, but in highly armed societies. The Cold War presented a fundamental paradox. Nuclear weapons had abolished hot war, and thus undermined the solidarity that comes from fighting a genuine enemy, but they did not produce peace. People lived in fear of a nuclear holocaust, a fear heightened during periods of tension between the blocs. This fear did not lead to national solidarity, but to a diffuse terror on the part of powerless individuals.

Hence the immense relief during the periodic 'thaws' during the Cold War and the tendency of the USA and USSR to return to dialogue and détente after relatively short periods of tension. The dialogue between Reagan and Gorbachev ended the Cold War and thus the fear of a generalized nuclear exchange. This reduction of nuclear tension continues, not because Russia has ceased to be a nuclear power, but because it has ceased to be an ideological one and because it is neither willing nor able to contend with the USA for world power. Russia's vital interests are currently confined within its own borders and in the 'near abroad'. It will only make serious nuclear threats if challenged on that terrain.

In the 1960s guerrilla warfare was seen by many commentators, left and right, military and political, as a new form of war that could take place despite the nuclear deadlock, and that threatened the West and its allies. It was directly linked to a new politics of national self-determination and anti-capitalist revolt in the periphery. In fact guerrilla war was not new. It was practised in Spain against Napoleon's armies. It relied then too on an asymmetry between local forces able to merge with the population and alien regular forces based in urban centres. As Mao in China and Giap in North Vietnam realized, such warfare could only be effective as a revolutionary tactic as part of a wider strategy of 'people's war'. This required that the political strength of the urban elite could be undermined, and, in consequence of such political defeat, that guerrilla tactics could be combined with those of a standing revolutionary army. It was this combination that led to Communist victory in the Chinese civil war in 1949 and to the collapse of the South Vietnamese state.

Guerrilla war is not an exclusive 'technology of the left'. It was used as a tactic by the American-supported rebels in Afghanistan, by Renamo in Mozambique, and by the Contras in Nicaragua. In each of these cases, rightist guerrillas, mostly professional mercenaries, enjoyed external support in pursuing a political strategy of using guerrilla tactics to destroy leftist 'civil society' in the countryside. The strategy was largely destructive, undermining health and education projects, and crippling agriculture. Leftist governments proved powerless to check them by conventional military methods and urban society proved too fragile a prop for the regime. Guerrilla war is a specific and limited form of war. Its success depends principally on the balance of political forces, and also on whether there is a powerful conventional 'sponsor', such as the Duke of Wellington in the Peninsula War or the Reagan government for the Contras. Guerrilla war became fashionable in the 1960s precisely because it was sponsored by the superpowers in their proxy struggles in the Cold War and also because of the stubborn resistance of states like France and Portugal to the end of colonialism.

Nuclear war, however, remained the dominant form of war, the one that shaped the core strategies of the most powerful states. Because nuclear war rendered war impossible between the advanced countries, it limited the direct impact of war on society. Mass mobilization of the home front was not required. The absence of conventional total war made possible a restoration of limited government in Western societies. The atomic bomb could in that sense be said to have made the world safe for liberalism, for without it the likelihood of a major conventional war between the superpowers in the half-century after 1945 was very high. Such a war would have probably kept the Soviet Union going. It would have provided a real enemy and thus a source of solidarity, and a situation in which a centralized command economy functions best. The current political situation is thus very much a product of the nuclear age. Nuclear weapons contributed significantly to the 'civilianization' of modern societies. Until nuclear weapons are diffused to other powers with intercontinental capacity and a reason to confront the USA, this is one of the fundamental continuities that carry forward into the twenty-first century.

The legacy of the military revolutions

There are other continuities that stretch even further back. From Cerignola to the Gulf the effects of successive military revolutions have been conserved within existing military systems. Conventional warfare has continued to exhibit a strong defensive bias based upon firepower. When in difficulty soldiers entrench and go underground. Permanent professional military forces remain. They are divided into units like battalions and companies, commanded by officers with traditional ranks like colonel and captain. Despite technological change, the basic infantry combat unit is still the battalion of 500–800 soldiers. Certain forms of organization thus remain tenacious. So, at the macro level, does the system of competing states. Indeed, it has been reinvigorated by the breakdown of the conflict between the superpower blocs. The USA is the sole remaining superpower, but its hegemony is neither comprehensive nor based on a project of direct conquest and control, unlike previous bids for power within the system by Spain, France and Germany. Since the industrial revolution changed war, it is transportation systems, communications technologies and weapons platforms that have been central to its effective conduct. This is even more the case today. Nuclear weapons are also still there in their silos and submarines.

However, just as the limitations on preindustrial war were removed by the industrial revolution, so some of the most constraining features of industrialized war are now passing away. During the Cold War mass armies based on conscription remained. Now they are obsolete in the advanced countries. The legacy of the *levée en masse* is over. Large numbers of soldiers with only basic skills and weapons add little to modern conventional war. Mass armies persisted in the advanced states because the Soviets still believed in the strategic offensive and the use of overwhelming numbers in successive waves. They kept reserve formations and obsolete weapons to throw in if needed, regardless of casualties. Western armies kept large orders of battle in order to respond to this threat.

Not only are mass armies obsolete in the advanced countries but so is that other feature of mass industrialization, total war. Total war was an effect of the stalemate on the battlefield. In a war of attrition the only option is to bleed the enemy into surrender, and to do so it is necessary to release as many combatants for the front and to produce as many weapons as possible. In order to do this civilian society must be militarized, all labour and resources being subject to central state control. All states adopted this strategy in the two world wars of this century. States, liberal and illiberal, were forced to use broadly similar methods. Indeed, the experience of 1914–18 convinced many that state socialism was both possible and efficient. This did not mean, as many believed in the 1930s, that authoritarian states were bound to be able to mobilize resources more efficiently than liberal ones and were thus likely to prevail over them. It turns out that total wars are not necessarily most effectively fought by totalitarian states. Nazi grand strategy and the German war economy were both badly managed. Liberal states proved more effective at managing total war economies than the fascist states. The reason is that they were able to rely on a combination of efficient, fair and lawful central state direction, the voluntary cooperation of big business in running the war effort, and a high level of support and sacrifice from citizens. In 1918 and 1945, war economies were more or less rapidly dismantled in the liberal states.

Such wars of attrition are currently less frequent. This is both because the disparity of forces is often such that wars are over rapidly, as with the Six Day War of 1967 in the Middle East, and because the political aims and, therefore, the military commitments of wars are more limited, as with NATO's campaign in Kosovo. Total war derived from military stalemate, but in the context of the goal of the total defeat of the enemy. Where both stalemate and unlimited war aims recur, as in the Iran–Iraq War, then so do some of the features of total war (although neither state was fully industrialized). Multistate wars will be unlikely to return to the scale of mass mobilization of 1939–45 for the foreseeable future, both because most of the states capable of fighting them are likely to have, or be capable of developing, weapons of mass destruction (no power with the nuclear bomb can lose a war of attrition), and because the economic and political causes of an unlimited conflict on the part of most major states do not currently exist. Either nuclear deterrence will cut in if there is an acute crisis, or the opposed parties will cut a deal. This means that, for the advanced states, we are returning for the next couple of decades at least to a condition rather like the liberal era for the Western powers between 1850 and 1890. States are limited governments; they make minimum military demands on their societies; the great powers will tend to cooperate in a crisis rather than fight; and the military will be subject to rapid technological change.

Since the sixteenth century the defensive, based on firepower, has tended to be by far the stronger form of war. This dominance of the defence has been punctuated by periods in which one state introduced new weapons and military methods that gave it a distinct but brief offensive advantage. Examples are the introduction of mass conscription in revolutionary France and German skill in mechanized warfare at the beginning of World War Two. These advantages have been rapidly removed as other states have adopted the same weapons and methods, or have used alternative means to counter them. Sometimes too there have been periods of major inequality in military power between different types of states, for example, that between European armies and non-European peoples in the period of high colonialism in the nineteenth century. The USA has a similar massive advantage today in both weapons and overall military skill over all other states. This is an unusually long period of offensive dominance for America and its allies. This may not last and changes in military technology may reinforce the defensive and thus reduce the offensive superiority of the USA.

War has a future. There is no danger of universal and perpetual peace breaking out in this century. Liberal states fight, they use force to impose their will. There will be multiple sources of conflict outside the advanced world. We shall return to the prospects of new wars and for yet another military revolution in chapter 3.

2

The International System in the Westphalian Era

The modern state and the modern international system developed together. Before the sixteenth century neither the sovereign territorial state nor a system of international politics based primarily upon such states existed. By the end of the seventeenth century both the system and a population of its member states were firmly established. The formation of states with exclusive control of a definite territory owed a great deal to the fact that they were members of an emerging international system that fostered and favoured such political entities. The characteristics of the state were shaped by the international system imposing norms from the beginning and also because the system selected out political entities that were so organized that they could not adapt to its constraints. The norms of the system rapidly came to favour coherent territorial entities that had a degree of effective control of the use of violence across their borders. Thus, from the beginning, territorial sovereignty has had a significant international dimension.

From medieval pluralism to the modern state

The modern state has three defining characteristics. First, it has a definite territory with boundaries at its exterior. Second, it has exclusive control of that territory: 'sovereignty' means that no other entity can substantiate a claim to rule in this space. Third, hierarchy, that is, the state is a superior political agency that determines the role and powers of all subsidiary governments.[1] The modern state developed on the basis of a few key centralizing medieval monarchies, chiefly England, France and Spain.[2] But in the late medieval period no state had developed these defining characteristics of territorial sovereignty.

Medieval Europe was a society made up of diverse political entities entering into complex mutual relations. There was thus no clear division between domestic politics and international relations. Across Europe boundaries were porous, ill-defined and seldom established by mutual recognition. Marchlands, disputed border zones, and shifting colonial frontiers were typical of the periphery, for example in Eastern Europe, between England and Scotland, and between Christian and Muslim Spain. Kings and leading nobles continuously disputed one another's right to territory and also inherited territory within the space of another kingdom. Many bodies claimed the key marks of sovereignty. These marks were, in the terms of the sixteenth-century French originator of the theory of state sovereignty, Jean Bodin, the power to make laws, to administer justice, to appoint lesser officers, to tax, to raise armies, to declare war, and to make treaties.[3] The sovereign, as sole and uncommanded commander, had no place in a political universe of parallel and competing powers,

each claiming and exercising similar rights. Medieval territories lacked not merely exclusive control by a single ruler
but also in most cases even the rudiments of a working
division of labour between different levels and types of
governance. Ruling powers competed to control the same
spaces, claiming forms of territorial and functionally
specific rule that were ill defined both in scope and rights.
Subjects owed different obligations to different rulers.
Status – whether that of the noble, serf, merchant, journey-
man, guild-master, monk or cleric – determined the law to
which one was subject and who exercised it.

Examples of these conflicting rights and obligations
abound. Thus the balance of power between the Holy
Roman Emperor and the disparate population of princely
states (some Electors with the right to appoint the
Emperor, some not), Imperial cities, prince bishoprics, and
free knights who made up the Empire was subject to
constant dispute and challenge. Pope and Emperor disputed the claim to be the principal ruler of Christendom.
Religious rulers, from the Pope to bishops, claimed and
exercised secular power. The Church claimed exclusive
governance of the religious, and extensive rights over the
laity, including the imposition of tithes and the power to
excommunicate. Monastic military orders like the Teu-
tonic Knights and the Hospitallers enjoyed not only the
right to act as armed powers on the periphery but to raise
money in Europe for their operations on its frontiers. City-
states and city leagues exercised functions that would later
be specific to states, such as raising armed forces, coining
money, declaring war and making treaties. Monarchs and
the greater feudal lords were not easily distinguished one
from another. The latter frequently sought to supplant or
to humble the former. In some realms, like Poland, king-
ship became elective, and in others, like Aragon, the king

could only rule by the consent of the nobility and on their terms.[4]

Medieval Europe was thus a complex political and social system that some commentators think mirrors the complex world of overlapping and competing governing powers of different types that they see as emerging today. The two periods of transition are reversed images of one another: one from pluralism and complexity to monopoly and simplicity in governance, and the other towards overlapping and competing authorities from the primacy of state power. How the first transition was effected may have lessons for the other, and our ability to determine whether or not it is taking place at all. Medieval Europe could have no clear distinction between domestic and foreign politics, and thus nothing resembling a proper international system. How this complex late medieval political system resolved itself into a relatively small core of territorial states is difficult to explain. It is especially difficult to do so if one relies primarily on causes and phenomena at the level of the individual state.

Explanations that are both general and parsimonious tend to be less than satisfying. Usually general models derived from political science come up against the complexities and contingencies of the process of state formation in individual countries. Most of the major states endured crises and radical reverses in the process of the centralization of sovereign power. Several nearly foundered more than once. State formation depended on the outcomes of internal struggles and external conflicts, and some political entities, apparently well favoured like Burgundy, failed to weather them. Some of this can only be explained by the fact that happenstance decided the outcome of closely matched contests.

There have been several recent well-developed attempts

to analyse the process of state formation and to explain the
main causal factors behind it. A good deal of scholarship
has seen war, and the military revolution in particular, as
central to this process of state formation. War created new
financial demands that only the central state could satisfy.
The appropriation of superior revenue-raising powers by
the central government was vital in its victory over lesser
authorities.[5] However, this is not to explain the process of
state-building, but mostly to redescribe success and to
ignore the fraught process by which many states came into
existence. In the middle of the religious civil wars in France
in the sixteenth century it would have been difficult to
ascribe any great superiority to the state in terms of
legitimacy, military capacity or revenue-raising power as
against the confessional factions. In the 1570s France
resembled the Lebanon in the mid-1970s. Numerous other
instances of the messy conflicts involved in state-building
contradict the notion that the central government had an
inherent superiority in warmaking or tax raising. We have
seen that this was not necessarily the case and that the new
weapons and tactics often enabled local powers and small
states to resist centralization and hegemonic bids for
power.

The Military Revolution has been seen by some political
scientists as the key explanatory factor, not only in the
process of state formation generally, but also in the types
of regime that eventuated. Brian M. Downing correlates
the key period of the formation of autocratic or representative governments with the advent of the military revolution in the period 1560–1660.[6] The difficulty with this
analysis is that it relies on a specific temporality for the
occurrence of the Military Revolution and the requirement
that its demands are such that they produce fiscal crisis.
Michael Roberts's 'Revolution' has been widely ques-
tioned; military change as we have seen was far more

complex in its temporality and its effects. 'Absolutism' was far from complete in practice.[7] For example, French absolutism never acquired a power to tax at will, despite intense pressures of military competition. The French state was limited by a complex structure of privileges and exemptions and the need to seek the consent of the Estates General for major new taxes. In the case of Denmark the advent of absolutism is closely connected to military defeat, but not especially to fiscal crisis. Rather it was the military incompetence of the traditional nobility, and defeat by Sweden, that led the King to abrogate noble rights and to centralize power, with widespread popular support.

The growing demand for revenue and political centralization is part of an accelerating process of interstate conflict that begins in the early sixteenth century and which stretches over the whole early modern period; it cannot easily be confined to the period of major constitutional changes in the seventeenth century. What does characterize that period is the crystallization of the new international system and the possibility of internal pacification. Thus states enjoyed the political space to engage in projects of appropriating sovereignty from lesser bodies.

The most important work attempting a general analysis of the rise of the modern state is Hendrik Spruyt's *The Sovereign State and its Competitors*.[8] This examines the rise of territorial sovereignty largely in terms of factors acting within the individual states. However, it has the great merit of asking an apparently simple question that others had failed to pose. Why was it that it was the sovereign territorial state that emerged as the dominant form of political organization from the crisis of the late medieval world rather than some other type of body? He makes it clear that there were competitors – effective forms of rule – for the role, such as the city-state, city leagues and

universal empires. Each was capable of overcoming the
political limits of feudal society. The crisis of late feudal
society is seen by Spruyt as a conflict between growing trade
and an urban society and the effects of a highly decentralized political system with parcellized sovereignty. The
emerging territorial monarchies are seen as the most appropriate solution for merchants seeking the greatest scope of
protection for the lowest cost of taxation. Competing local
powers multiply customs dues and offer less security. The
main problem with this analysis, apart from the rational
choice assumptions which hardly fit the motivations of elites
at the time, is that such uniformity was not achieved in
many of the core sovereign states. Thus France remained in
fact a patchwork of local powers, with numerous internal
customs barriers, up to the revolution of 1789.

Spruyt's approach is useful nevertheless in focusing on
the issue of why bodies like the Hanseatic League or major
city-states like Florence did not continue to grow in power
and retain their autonomy in relation to sovereigns. Here
we shall consider as an example the Hanseatic League,
which was a prime contender to be a rival form of large-
scale political organization to the territorial state.[9] In many
ways the League looks like a suprisingly modern organization, echoing forms of supranational governance today.
Founded in 1356, the League was a confederation of
northern European trading cities linked by common mer-
cantile practices, which had established its own common
trading counters across Europe. Its key cities were connected by a set of common institutions and decision procedures and it spanned the territories of what were or were
to become distinct states such as Prussia, Poland and
Sweden. The League signed treaties with monarchs,
obtained extraterritorial privileges for its trading outposts
in countries like England, and used armed force to enforce
its collective will. It was a quasi-polity with common but

functionally limited institutions, whose members were self-governing entities in their own right. It depended on the wealth and military power of a small number of its leading cities, chief of which was Lübeck. It operated on a European scale and had resources superior to those of many monarchs. Some commentators have seen it as a political model that may be useful as a way of thinking about the European Union.[10]

The League suffered from four principal weaknesses that led to its gradual marginalization as a player in the emerging international system until it was disbanded in 1669. First, its decision procedures were cumbersome and it was faced with a problem of free riding, as lesser cities relied on a few major cities like Lübeck to provide the bulk of its military forces. Second, it was mainly an economic organization and thus its concerns became less central as religious issues came to dominate its heartland in Germany after the Reformation. The League's cities were mainly Protestant and thus it was caught in the middle of the confessional conflicts without being a decisive player in them. Third, in the sixteenth century it faced territorially based commercial competitors; its commercial monopolies were challenged by the Dutch and its exclusive trading concessions were repudiated by England. The League found it harder to enforce its commercial position with force. It suffered from the fact that, as the sixteenth century unfolded, merchant ships and warships diverged from each other in type. This meant that it was harder to convert commercial strength directly into military strength. This increased the cost of defending its trading position and increased the strain on the leading members of the League, thus reducing their willingness to tolerate free riders. Fourth, as territorial powers began to consolidate, as in Brandenburg and Sweden, the cities of the League were increasingly subject to the external policy of their monarchs. The supraterritoriality of the League became a disadvantage the more the principle of territorial sovereignty took hold. It had no potential hinterland that it could use as a base to rival the other powers at their own game, as Venice did with the acquisition of territory on the mainland, the *terra firma*. The League's fundamental principles of governance relied on a European political system that was not territorially exclusive, in which political as well as trade links could be forged between cities within and outside the nominal sovereignty of the Empire.

Before exclusive territoriality took hold the forms of political identification we take to be normal did not exist. Rulers and ruled were often quite different in language, ethnicity, culture and religion. Loyalties could be divided, just as sovereignty was parcellized. Individuals could find their estate, confessional group, guild or city the primary focus of their political loyalty. Rulers thus did not begin with a decisive cultural or ideological advantage over other groups in the construction of exclusive control of a territory. Indeed, the Reformation, in creating 'ideology' (that is, the derivation of politics from doctrine and the willingness to use force to promote doctrine), challenged those fragile forms of proto-national identification that were emerging, for example in England and France during the Hundred Years' War.

State-building required the suppression of religious conflict. First, state and religion were identified with each other in those countries where one religious party was the clear victor in the sixteenth century. Political power became the shell for a new religious constitution, identified by its supporters with religious freedom. In fact, the union between state and religion was forged in political struggle, and the price of freedom for some was that dissenting voices were suppressed or expelled. Thus John Knox and the Scottish Calvinist elites forged the notion of the Scots as a 'Covenanted Godly People' by the systematic repression of opponents. England became a militantly Protestant state during its war with Spain and cracked down on Catholics. Likewise, policies of religious police and the suppression of heretics were practised in Catholic Spain and by the Counter-Reformation Papacy. Then, second, the widespread stabilization of confessional territories and an end to the religious civil wars, particularly as an effect of the Peace of Westphalia, enabled other states to begin to gain control of their populations, but also to build new forms of political identification for them.

Given the suppression of internal conflicts, first in the form of an exclusive identification between religion and territory, it then became possible to build other and wider forms of identification between rulers and ruled. The notion that rulers and people should be alike, except in their political functions, that they should share a distinct homeland and a common culture, is a modern one. Once the state contains internal rebellion and eliminates rival centres of power, then it can begin to build new forms of identification for subjects that locate enemies outside, in other states. As this happened it became necessary to include the ruled, at least rhetorically, within the political community. It was a central project of modern state-building to accomplish this. Such homogeneity tied people to the state territory and provided a powerful legitimation for why there should be an exclusive power ruling that space. Without the territorialization of political power it is difficult to imagine the gradual process of the identification of state and society. The fusion of state and society in a 'country' like France or Britain is not, as some globalization theorists imagine, an aberration of social scientists, but a politically constructed reality, and the foundation for modern nationalism and democracy.

If one assumes the success of this political project of the

concentration of political power and its legitimation, then territorial states had real advantages over other forms of political organisation. However, such processes of political identification were seldom fully realized in the first half of the seventeenth century. In particular, it was difficult to achieve minimum stability if other powers were engaged in a pan-European ideological conflict by aiding confessional rebels within the state's borders. The states that failed in this project of building identification on the part of their peoples, and therefore political legitimacy, were those that ultimately failed to become territorial powers or to survive as such.

The emerging international system

The emerging international system was aided in its formation both by the overriding necessity to territorialize religion, and by the will-to-power of state elites in the new wars of the sixteenth century. These wars had been initiated by ambitious centralizing monarchs and had been given a religious dimension beyond the control of elites in the struggles in northern Europe. The new system was structured by two basic principles, both of which – when they could be actualized – favoured the sovereign territorial state.[11]

The first principle is *exclusion*. All entities that are not coherently territorial and exclusively sovereign within are progressively delegitimated and expelled from the international system. The chief victims were those political bodies that had been parts of the old Christian Commonwealth of Europe along with the monarchs and princes. Thus the Church as a pan-European institution, the monastic military orders, the Hanseatic League and the

city-state were all either eliminated or marginalized as
international players in the course of the seventeenth century. Both the League and the Papacy had no part in the
peace process of Westphalia, having previously been major
powers in the German lands. The interests of the League
were represented by Lübeck, which had standing within
the Imperial constitution. Most treaties are complex com-
promises, syntheses of conflicting interests, and Westphalia
was especially so, the negotiations being fraught and prolonged. It was driven by political necessities in which the
Church and the League as supra-German institutions on
opposite sides of the religious fence could have no useful
part and in which they would both lose from the terms of
the settlement. The Pope was appalled by the outcome
and produced a furious Bull lambasting the Catholic powers in Germany for conceding in effect the legitimacy of
the Protestant rulers.

The Holy Roman Empire, the other prime loser with
the Papacy in 1648, was reduced by the outcome of the
Thirty Years' War to a hollow political shell in which the
various German states came to enjoy a degree of sovereignty just short of complete independence. The Empire
lingered on, increasingly marginal in relation to the major
territorial states, like Austria, Brandenburg-Prussia, and
Saxony, until abolished by Napoleon in 1806. Likewise,
the Hospitallers, having played a vital role in resisting the
Ottoman advance in the Mediterranean and based on the
strategically significant island of Malta, became an increasingly honorific irrelevance in the European states system
until abolished by Napoleon. The same could be said of
Venice, until the Republic was dissolved by the French
revolutionary government at the end of the eighteenth
century. The reason that the French were the liquidators
of many of these institutional relics was that they were
bound neither by tradition nor dynastic protocol. The

Treaty of Westphalia had tended to freeze the political/
religious status quo within the German lands and thus to
preserve political entities that had become obsolete. Exclusion is thus a process that takes place at the international
level, corresponding in many ways to the process within
states whereby elements of sovereignty were appropriated
from other bodies. This principle of exclusion continued
to operate throughout the Westphalian era down to 1914.
It began in Europe but was then extended throughout the
world as European states seized their colonial empires.

The second constitutive principle of the new international system is *mutual recognition*.[12] Legitimate membership of the system depended on acceptance by other states
as the exclusive ruler of a definite territory. A defining
feature of modern sovereignty is the recognition by states
of the difference between internal and external policy, and
thus arises the norm of non-interference in the internal
affairs of other states. Interaction between states should
take place at their borders in the trinity of commerce,
diplomacy and war. This principle was first accepted internationally in matters of religion in the provisions of the
Treaty of Westphalia. It is worth spelling out in some more
detail why the norm of non-interference should begin with
religious matters. The object of the treaty was to reaffirm
the terms of the purely German religious peace of 1555,
which had broken down and led to foreign intervention.
This settlement had tried to confessionalize the states of
the Empire into Catholic and Protestant on the pragmatic
maxim of *cuius regio eius religio*, that is, that the religion of
the ruling prince is the religion of the state. To restore this
in 1648 it was necessary to get the powers that had
intervened in Germany, chiefly France and Sweden, to
underwrite this settlement and not to attempt to alter it.
To make territorialization acceptable to the losers and to
prevent future conflicts, the treaty established the first

internationally recognized 'human right', to leave a state whose established religion one dissented from. Religion then being the dominant human concern and the Empire the cockpit of the European religious struggles, these provisions of the treaty had a major constitutive effect on the European states system. Not only did it enable states effectively to assert sovereignty within, but it also structured the character of competition between states.

It has become fashionable among some international relations theorists to talk down the centrality of Westphalia, chiefly because many of the features of the old European order persisted for some time after it.[13] However, Westphalia is central in initiating the double depoliticization that structures the international system up to 1914. The first depoliticization is internal: by increasing acceptance of the norm of non-intervention, states enabled each other to gain control of their societies and to considerably reduce the level of their internal conflicts. Thus they could acquire a monopoly of the means of violence and begin to build new forms of identification with their peoples. The second depoliticization is external. States eschewed ideology as the principle of their relations in favour of the primacy of reason of state. Interstate relations could, therefore, be primarily a matter of the balance of power and the acquisition of territory in Europe and colonies abroad.

States have never been pure billiard balls, interacting in a situation of international anarchy and lawlessness. The central norms of the international system – non-interference in the internal affairs of other states, no territory without a single legitimate ruler, and the legitimacy of reason of state as the foundation of external policy – are those that are peculiar to states. Reason of state is thus part of a normative order, despite its rejection of substantive values in favour of political calculation based exclusively on morally neutral power technique. In the sixteenth

century reason of state was the core legitimation for the
pursuit of power within states, as well as in international
conflicts. It could thus appear as a genuine political doctrine and not merely as a cover for an amoral Machiavellian
policy on the part of princes. The reason for this valoriza-
tion of reason of state is that key intellectuals and elites
had come to see the state as the essential source of security
and stability, the only power that could contain the vicious
religious conflicts in contemporary society. Jean Bodin and
Thomas Hobbes, the key creators of the modern theory of
state sovereignty, both came to believe that enforced out-
ward conformity in religious belief was a virtue. Political
dissent in religious matters led to chaos. It undermined
not merely public peace but Christianity itself, since
unspeakable acts were committed in its name. For peace
to exist there could be no power, internal or external, to
set against the sovereign and no legitimate action in politics
other than by the sovereign's will. Thus a principled
justification was provided for the appropriation of power
by, and its concentration in the hands of, the central state.

Carl Schmitt and Reinhard Koselleck have enabled us
to recover the full meaning of this key moment in the
invention of modern sovereignty.[14] The thinkers of the
Enlightenment would come to see reason of state as cynical
and as not merely morally neutral but immoral. In a period
of relative social stability during the ancien régime it would
no longer be understood as a constitutive depoliticization
necessary to that very security. For the thinkers of the
Enlightenment 'civil society' (even if they did not have the
concept in the modern, Hegelian sense) was the source of
all that was healthy in the political world. The state should
be subordinate to society and it should not pursue international power struggles for their own sake. This Enlightenment attitude seems to Schmitt to be wishful thinking.
For him the essence of politics is friend–enemy relations,

conflicts over substantive issues that group the protagonists into irreconcilable opponents. States limit enmity within. For Schmitt sovereignty is the ability of the victors to contain conflicts and to depoliticize domestic society. States also structure and, therefore, limit conflict without. Only state officials decide whether to make war on other states.

Reason of state is founded on the core assumptions of realism as a discourse on foreign policy. Those assumptions are that conflicts are mainly phenomena generated by factors within the international system, that states are the primary actors in that system, and that member states of the system may be friends or enemies in the future as circumstances dictate. It has become fashionable to criticize realism and its modern derivatives as a theory in the discipline of international relations, but we consider it here as a core set of maxims of statecraft in a system of competing states.[15] Reason of state limits the enmity of interstate relations in that it makes them a matter of pure power technique: one's enemy is not an implacable foe but an honourable opponent in a conflict of interests.

Realism has the advantage that it does not require leaders to convert the personnel of enemy states into moral inferiors. Providing they abide by the fundamental norms of the international system, other states can be dealt with as legitimate opponents. Realism also treats international politics as a matter managed by states. Societies and ordinary civilians should keep out of such conflicts and persons only appear in them as servants of the state. Thus reason of state, by depoliticizing conflicts, made it possible for civilians to appear in them as neutrals.

The moral neutrality inherent in reason of state is thus capable of justification in both its domestic and international aspects. But depoliticization was only one aspect of the process of building state sovereignty. After the mid-seventeenth century states go a long way to externalizing conflict, fighting a succession of wars with one another. One of the effects of almost continuous war is that states can construct a new loyalty on the part of their subjects by focusing on external enemies. The externalization of enmity could not be switched on and off so easily as the dictates of realist statecraft might decree. As part of the process of tying rulers and ruled together discussed above, it led ultimately to nationalism and to popular support for aggression against foreign peoples defined as natural enemies. In this sense nationalism cut across the Enlightenment belief that civil society would check the aggression of aristocratic elites if it were to be given political expression in representative government. Nationalism and liberalism were different principles of legitimation and could well conflict.

The other aspect of seventeenth-century state-building that complicates pure realism in the conduct of international affairs is the 'discovery of the economy' by ruling elites. The creation of exclusively governed distinct territories is a precondition for the notion of a 'national economy'. The result is the widespread adoption of mercantilist doctrines and practices in mid seventeenth-century Europe. States aimed to maximize the supply of gold in their territories and thus to increase their potential revenues. Money is power because it can buy the means of external aggression. The state also needs to ensure the domestic supply of resources that can be purchased with money. Thus the state becomes a utility maximizer. The way to do so is seen to be by increasing the nation's share of total foreign trade and making sure that that trade is in the hands of its own subjects. Hence the English Navigation Acts and the attempt by Louis XIV's minister Colbert to boost the manufactures, foreign trade and merchant marine of France. Such economic constraints meant that rulers had to adopt a distinct domain of rationality, economics, into the calculations of reason of state. Rulers had to attend to the economic effects of their policies and thus to the 'economy' as a distinct sphere of action that is the object of state policy but not reducible to it. Policy required a new kind of prudence. The state disempowered itself if its policies reduced the wealth of society. Thus the indirect effect of mercantilism was ultimately to create political economy, the science of the maximization of national wealth. Economics is thus political in origin; it could not come into existence until the economy emerged as an object of policy, and that could not happen until the central state monopolized certain functions.

Mercantilism, by regulating commerce between nations and seeking to maximize the state's share of international trade, thus created a new and distinct cause of war in commercial competition. The Anglo-Dutch wars of the seventeenth century were mercantilist wars pure and simple, between states that had hitherto been allies in the religious wars. England's conflicts with France and Spain were driven by balance of power considerations, but central in them was the struggle to secure dominance in carrying the commerce of the world to Europe.

The rise of liberalism

The modern states system thus began on the basis of three components, each of which emphasized territorial exclusiveness – internal pacification, the dynasticization of legitimacy and mercantilism. Very little of a suprastate order could be raised on these foundations, other than the common manners of European aristocratic elites. European politics were transformed in the 'long nineteenth

century' from 1815 to 1914 by three quite different forces
– nationalism, conservatism and liberalism. Nationalism
rearranged the membership of the states system through a
politics of unification and secession. However, nationalism
merely replaced one principle of legitimacy with another
and stronger one, substituting for loyalty to the Crown and
the religious constitution that of membership of the
'nation'.

Conservatism did provide a new basis for supranational
order. The peace settlement of Vienna in 1815 created the
Concert of Europe. This was based on the alliance of
powers that had defeated Napoleon, but included the
newly restored monarchy in France. This marked a significant change from the shifting alliances and balance of
power struggles that had characterized the international
politics of European dynastic states in the eighteenth century. The balance in interstate politics shifted from conflict
to explicit and relatively durable cooperation. The aim of
this cooperation was to avoid major conflicts and to intervene in the conflicts of lesser states in order to preserve
stability and to limit the opportunities for revolutionary
forces to seize power. The interstate collaboration of the
Concert of Europe was resurrected in one form or another
throughout the nineteenth century. Conservatism also
involved a closer form of cooperation, that between Austria, Prussia and Russia. This policy was orchestrated first
by the Austrian chancellor Metternich, who coordinated
the rigorous suppression of democratic movements. Cooperation between the three powers was decisive in frustrat-
ing the revolutions in Austria, Germany, Italy and Hungary
in 1848. The three powers revived their cooperation after
the formation of the German Empire in 1871. Bismarck,
the German chancellor, saw this as the foundation of
stability in Europe and it persisted until the early 1890s.
Then divergent national interests overcame the common

conservative concern with preventing revolution. Germany and Russia became part of distinct alliances, with the latter tied to the former's principal rival, France. While cooperation between the Great Powers declined as their national rivalries rose, even so they continued to try to reconcile differences and to contain lesser conflicts up to the outbreak of war in 1914.

The Concert of Europe relied on explicit cooperation by political leaders. Liberalism, by contrast, was a political and economic doctrine that could create a relatively durable international order beyond the state.[16] Liberalism relied on explicit state policies to create and sustain it, but it did open up a realm of non-state activity that tied nations together. Liberalism redefined the functions of the state: it was a doubly limited government that existed to secure the private purposes of citizens in domestic civil society and to protect the private international commerce of individuals. Other contemporary political projects, including radical democracy, defined themselves within the boundaries of a symbolic state territory. Socialism, which developed to challenge liberalism, preached internationalism, but it had no coherent vision of an international order. In fact socialism was resolutely nationalist in that it depended on harnessing the power of the state to its programme of curtailing private property. Liberals did have such a vision. Their international order was to be based on the free commerce of individuals, and the principal legitimate external role of states was to make this possible. Liberalism as a mature political form is defined by a double limitation of the scope of government. First, the state is separate from a largely self-regulating 'civil society', a domain of private exchange and free association that it exists to guarantee and secure. Second, the state allows individuals to trade and to travel freely across its borders, and extends this right both to citizens and foreigners. It is thus a local guardian of the world republic of commerce. The state should in consequence limit its external use of force against other states and persons to the enforcement of international norms, to protecting its citizens' rights and property abroad, and to the defence of its own territorial integrity. *Laissez-faire* and *laissez-passer* were the watchwords of the new state. The limitation of the aims of government did not mean that the scope of government was restricted or that the state was weak. Liberal states intervened in all social spheres to ensure that social agents conformed to the new social order and they used force to create and to defend the new international order.[17]

A kind of liberalism, in the sense of limited government, was built from the beginning into the theoretical defence by Hobbes and others of the sovereign state as the protector of public peace. But in the late eighteenth century liberalism was redefined by a number of key thinkers as a doctrine with a strong international dimension. The 'discovery of the economy' extends beyond the boundaries of the nation to the international trading system as an object of public policy, requiring appropriate action by the member states. Economic liberalism from Adam Smith onwards argues that the state should extend the freedom of private action to the economy, placing as few limits on domestic and foreign commerce as possible – basically those that are necessary to public safety and morality. The monopoly trading companies of the mercantilist era limited the growth of general wealth by restricting opportunities to trade in the interests of state-sanctioned private profit. The maximization of utility recognizes no difference between nationals and foreigners: both should be free to trade and the state should open its borders to the free circulation of goods. International political liberalism from Kant onwards contends that the external actions of states need positive legitimation as much as their domestic ones; reason of state will no longer do.[18] This can only be done by making them subject to the consent of citizens through their representatives. Governments should be 'republican', answerable to the representatives of civil society, and external policy should be subject to the test that it conforms to the interests of citizens. States should not practise aggressive war and should, if liberal, join a federation of free states committed to the principle that they will fight only if attacked.

An international liberal order was only fully established in the second half of the nineteenth century. It depended crucially on the policy of Britain as the leading commercial, industrial and naval power. However, most of the leading states of Europe shared the basic features of liberal society, even if several were slow in developing liberal polities with full representative government. Even though several states, including Germany, imposed protective tariffs after 1870, this did not halt the growth in international trade. Most of the major states were participants in the liberal era, even if some exhibited autocratic features. Russia, with its extensive controls on internal and external travel and commerce, was seen by a wide spectrum of opinion in Western Europe as despotic and backward.

Liberalism relied on force, both to clear the way for self-regulating institutions and to protect them from challenge. Britain created a new international order based on free trade after 1850. This involved forcing non-European states to accept the freedom of private commerce. It also involved a high degree of asymmetry, maintaining free trade even when states such as Germany and the USA imposed tariffs on commerce. The Gold Standard, the international monetary system widely adopted after 1870, was sustained by the policies of the Bank of England and by Britain's deep financial markets.[19] Britain and as the leading international lenders, acted to enforce proFrance,

bity on defaulting governments such as Egypt and Mexico.
Unlike the IMF, which sends a few economists with lap-
tops, creditor governments relied on military sanctions and
the direct administration of state revenues.

In many ways the international economy of the *belle
époque* from 1850 to 1914 resembled that of today. By
1914, most major states, with the exception of the USA,
had developed merchandise trade to GDP ratios compar-
able to those of today or greater. The UK had a ratio of
44.7 per cent in 1913 as against 42.6 per cent in 1994.
France had a ratio of 35.4 per cent in 1913 as against 36.6
per cent in 1995 and Germany 35.1 per cent in contrast to
the slightly larger figure of 38.7 per cent for 1995.[20] Levels
of capital export were proportionally as high or higher for
most major creditor nations than today. Thus the UK
exported capital to the value of 4.6 per cent of GDP on
average in the period 1890–1914 as against 2.6 per cent in
1990–6. The figures for France are 1.3 per cent in the
earlier period as against 0.7 per cent in the later one.[21] It
was the nineteenth century that was the true age of mass
migration. Surplus labour moved from Europe to build the
'neo-Europes' of the Americas, Africa and Australasia.
Some 60 million voluntary migrants left Europe to settle
permanently in the century after 1815. There were also
large flows of voluntary and involuntary labour from Africa
and Asia.

Europe created a world economy in the nineteenth
century by exporting capital and labour and by unparal-
leled colonial expansion. Liberals came to see this process
as a natural phenomenon, rather than as the product of a
certain balance of military and economic power. Many
liberals before 1914 saw the highly integrated international
economy and the commercial civilization that went along
with it as infinitely extendable and durable, much as the

advocates of 'globalization' among the international technocracy and business class do today. The consequences of 1914 and 1929 should remind us that such international orders are neither natural nor permanent, but are sustained by a mixture of economic circumstances, the policy of the leading states, and force.

International norms and conflicting nations

The century after 1815 could be termed the Clausewitz–Cobden era from the leading thinkers who defined the two main forms of interaction between states, war and trade. For Clausewitz the international system was made up exclusively of sovereign states interacting in terms of foreign policy. Wars were accepted by rulers as a legitimate means of settling what were otherwise intractable interstate disputes. The decision to go to war, however, was under clear political control. The conduct of war was subject to political limitations and norms. Although the Great Powers in this period sought to avoid going to war one with another, all the major states fought wars with their equivalents, except the USA. War was the continuation of policy by other means in Clausewitz's terms and regarded as, in the right circumstances, a morally neutral means of settling disputes. Wars between the major powers were conducted by organized armies, and the military generally respected the non-combatant status of civilians. In the colonies and against non-European peoples things were very different. International law was seen to apply fully only to European states and their derivatives, and the laws of war to apply only in conflicts between 'civilized' peoples. Clausewitz set his ideas about the decisive nature of military operations in the context of political limitation, that of the European *Rechtsstaat*.

Richard Cobden, the leading British advocate of free trade, supported international liberalism. International commerce was a matter of free exchange between individuals and states should not directly intervene in it. War and economics were separate spheres of activity. War was 'a duel between governments'.[22] States and civil societies were to be separated across borders as well as within them. States should, therefore, interfere as little as possible in the free flow of commerce even in time of war. Cobden, like many liberals, defined war narrowly and redefined the use of force otherwise as police action. Force was legitimate against pirates and also against states that tried to interfere with the rights of free trade and private property. In this sense he was like many modern advocates of the armed enforcement of human rights, who see such action not as war but as measures to deal with criminals and enemies of humankind.

The economic and political components of the Clausewitz–Cobden system were thus different, if structurally compatible. In matters of war and peace states were part of an international system in which they were the definitive agents. They had the option of pursuing an autonomous external policy, determined by domestic political leaders. In matters of commerce states accepted the existence of an international civil society of private exchanges and increasingly applied their sovereign power to promoting and protecting trade. The international system was still dominated by states, yet in many ways those states were almost as constrained by supranational forces as states are today. For all their formal political autonomy, states were rule followers. A *Rechtsstaat* within, the state abided by the norms of the international system without.

The liberal era required states to conform to a thick
script of international norms in their internal and external
dealings. States were only accepted as sovereign if they
behaved in certain ways. Free commerce between states
forced the international community of the day to define
what were legitimate objects of commerce and trade practices. States had to protect the property of foreign citizens,
to accept the right to foreign trade, to prohibit and sup-
press the slave trade, to take measures against piracy, and
to prevent mercenary adventures from their soil against
other legitimate states.[23] Political entities that did not
conform to these norms or to the structural features of
liberal sovereignty, like the Dey of Algiers in harbouring
pirates, or the Chinese and Japanese empires in refusing
British trade, were subject to armed sanctions.

Interstate collaboration in the interests of peace and
Great Power actions in pursuit of human rights are not
peculiarities of the post-Cold War era. Indeed, some of the
features of the liberal era in the long nineteenth century
seem to be returning today. The collaboration of the Great
Powers was essentially conservative, but it did take account
of human rights to some extent. Reason of state was no
longer supreme, politicians had to take account of citizens
and the new media of newspapers and the telegraph. The
powers could be spurred to act by public opinion. Thus
pure reason of state was tempered by common moral
sentiments. Realpolitik and morality could get mixed up,
much like today. The liberal powers, Britain and France,
were the most sympathetic to the rights of nations to self-
determination, but liberal opinion throughout Europe supported the struggle of suppressed nations for freedom from
Ottoman rule. Similarly, slavery was widely regarded as an
abomination. Britain ensured that the slave trade became
illegal. Slavers could be lawfully searched and seized upon
the high seas. In the Balkans the European powers tried to

prevent each other from deriving too much benefit from Ottoman collapse, and to contain conflicts between Balkan rivals, but they also aided the national liberation movements. Thus Britain, France and Russia intervened in favour of the Greeks at Navarino in 1827, destroying the Ottoman fleet. At the Congress of Berlin in 1878 the Great Powers sought to limit Russian gains but also to adjust and to stabilize the borders of the states emerging from Ottoman rule. The Treaty of London, of 1913, tried to do the same in the aftermath of the Balkan war of 1912. It failed and led to a new conflict. The modern Great Powers' attempts to end Balkan conflicts at Dayton and Rambouillet are thus far less remarkable than they may seem. We are, at the beginning of the twenty-first century, apparently going back to a liberal international order in which the powers have mixed motives. Cynicism and righteous intervention go hand in hand. The opponents of slavery and the supporters of nationality in the nineteenth century were the human rights activists of their day. Rights are not new in international politics, it is their content that differs.

The First World War destroyed the Clausewitzian–Cobdenite system. It undermined limited government within states in the pursuit of total war. Total war also destroyed the liberal international order. States practised autarchy as far as they could: regulating foreign trade, controlling shipping, ending the convertibility of currencies, and practising economic warfare one upon another. The scale and duration of the war damaged the legitimacy of war as a morally neutral power technique in relations between states, especially among the publics of the Allied powers. Thus resulted that peculiar mixture of the aims of US President Woodrow Wilson and the French Premier Georges Clemenceau that characterized the Versailles peace settlement in 1919. The French were foremost in demanding the recognition of German war guilt, disarmament of Germany, and the payment of punitive reparations. Wilson was the prime mover in demanding the recognition of national self-determination in the break-up of the old empires and the creation of a postwar system of collective security based on a new organ of international government, the League of Nations. The United States subsequently failed to ratify membership of the League, thus undermining it. However, the 1919 settlement included elements of international recognition of human rights, in the form of the protection of minority rights by the international community in the newly independent states of Eastern Europe. It also ended the practice of transferring colonies from the vanquished to the victors, without regard to the interests or wishes of the colonized. Germany's colonies were placed under French and British administration as mandated territories of the League.

In the aftermath of 1918 the victors tried to put the old liberal pre-1914 international economic order back together again, returning to free trade and seeking to restore the Gold Standard. This failed completely in the aftermath of the 1929 crash. This led directly to the widespread adoption of protectionism, the collapse of convertibility, and, on the part of the 'have not' states – Germany, Italy and Japan – the objective of bringing foreign markets and raw materials under their political control. The 1930s involved a major step back from international economic liberalism.

The crash of 1929 made the social conflicts that had emerged with a greater or lesser degree of severity in most of the industrial states after 1918 an international issue. Communism and fascism created a new era of ideological civil wars that cut across national borders and that ideologized international conflicts. Communism, fascism and liberalism struggled for international hegemony. In the 1930s it looked to many as if liberalism was likely to be the loser.[24] The Second World War became a fight for survival between states and ideologies. This conflict broke through the limits of the Clausewitzian military system. War now had unlimited objectives: policy required absolute war and the elimination of the enemy. The logic of war to ascend to the extreme was doubled by the logic of extreme political goals. This was as true of the liberal states as of the Nazis. They demanded the unconditional surrender of the Axis powers. By waging aggressive war the fascist powers had forfeited the right to exist as states. The liberal powers waged war ruthlessly, using indiscriminate bombing of civilian targets, unrestricted submarine warfare, and the atomic bomb. The liberal states were on the victorious side and military victory relegitimated Anglo-American values. Military defeat destroyed the credibility of fascism, because it had staked so much on the superior efficiency and military prowess of the authoritarian regimes.

The defeat of fascism, American hegemony and the atomic bomb contained postwar ideological conflict. Ideology now became a dimension in the conflict between two blocs of states. Each eliminated internal dissent. The Soviets did so brutally, the Americans by the more limited means of McCarthyism at home and coups abroad. Communism no longer appealed to more than a containable minority in the West. The Cold War was not like the ideological wars of religion or the 1930s; international conflict was not doubled and reinforced by civil war in the core of the two blocs. But both fought wars by proxy, intervening in and fomenting civil wars in peripheral regions throughout the globe. The Cold War both reconfigured the international system, forcing states into blocs dominated by the superpowers, and gave enhanced saliency to the sovereign state. States mattered: they were the necessary means of buying the loyalty of populations through managed economic growth and welfare services, and they were also valuable as allies, as loyal parts of the Free World or International Communism. The superpowers needed their allied nation-states as more than mere clients. The Soviets' problem was that most of their states were just that and the ones that were not were headaches, like Yugoslavia, China or Romania.

Why was the outcome in 1945 so different from that of 1918? American dominance was common to the aftermath of both wars, with the Western European states enfeebled and indebted. The presence of the Soviet Union certainly provided a spur towards a more interventionist and less isolationist policy on the part of the USA. However, the two great wars of the twentieth century had led to a retreat from international economic liberalism and to a 'nationalization' of the economy. This was both because of their effects in curtailing trade and because of the reinforcement of state economic management through war economy measures.

The first reason why the postwar planning of the international order in 1944–5 was very different in its outcome is because the struggle between democracy and fascism changed the terms of the relationship between victorious and defeated states. In 1919 harsh terms were imposed on Germany, but it was left to create its own domestic regime. That the existing states of Germany and Japan in 1945 were to be destroyed paradoxically made possible the Allied reconstruction of the economies and societies of these countries. Without a large measure of control over these countries' institutions and governance, the level of US aid and technology transfer that turned both into industrial competitors of American manufacturers would have been unlikely to have taken place. The next two most powerful economies of the contemporary G7 group of industrial nations after the USA were enabled to rebuild themselves as full members of an open international econ-

omy. American military might defended them and US
military aid enabled them to rearm at low cost. Both
countries, from having been inefficient militaristic economies in the 1930s, enjoyed the benefit of low ratios of
military spending to GDP.

The other reason is because the war led to a break-
through of Keynesian ideas with key government elites in
the UK and USA. Keynesianism is normally seen as a
technique of national economic management, especially
among those who see globalization as undermining the
postwar 'Keynesian welfare state', but these ideas were
central in making possible the Bretton Woods settlement.
The architects of the new institutions had the confidence
to rebuild an open world economy precisely because they
had techniques of economic management at the national
level that could ensure sustained output and high employment. National policy could thus contain and reverse
international shocks, preventing the downward spiral and
trade-reducing national policies of the 1930s. Keynesian
policies were a form of liberal collectivism that avoided the
stark alternatives of state-directed autarchy and unstable
laissez-faire. Governments since have tried to maintain this
balance of internal and external policy – even the disastrous experiment with monetarism was an attempt at activist national policies to contain inflation while preserving
domestic growth in an open economy. In that sense, as we
shall see in chapter 4, the balancing act between national
economic management and international openness continues until the present day.

The USA was thus far more successful at building its
international order than was the USSR. The international
economic institutions created under American hegemony
after 1945 proved durable and created a level of supranational governance that had never really existed before.[25]
They were of course dependent on the support of state

power for their effective functioning. American supremacy made it possible for the USA to underwrite the new international monetary system designed at Bretton Woods, its stability based on the convertibility of the dollar into gold, but supported by the International Monetary Fund (IMF) as the means to overcome balance of payments crises and thus to sustain trade. The USA initiated the return to free trade under the General Agreement on Tariffs and Trade (GATT). It also facilitated large-scale economic aid to developing economies through the creation of the World Bank. The very asymmetry of power made it possible to restart the international system with a relatively coherent architecture, much as the economic dominance of Britain after 1815 enabled it to shape the Pax Britannica.

The new system was very different from the pre-1914 world. It ceased to be just a world of states. The creation of the IMF, the World Bank, and GATT, and later the G7, created standing institutions of governance that had a more profound effect in changing the international system than did the other post-1945 creation, the United Nations and its agencies. The US was central to creating and sustaining this international economic system but it was not above it. It was bound by the rules of the new system. With the recovery and growth of the major states and the rapid growth of international trade, and with the relative decline of the USA (as compared with the immediate postwar period, it is now hegemonic on some dimensions but not on others), this standing system of international institutions has consolidated to the point that it has become a quasi-polity of which the major industrial states are members. States now govern the international economy in partnership with supranational institutions.

We have returned to a Cobdenite world to the extent that states are limited governments in a free trading sys-

tem, but with the difference that the system is now extensively governed by supranational institutions. What then of
war? Will the new power relations restore Clausewitzian
war in the sense that war is a continuation of policy, or will
they create new forms of conflict that undermine the
control of war by the state?

Before we turn to consider these questions about the
future in the next two chapters it may be useful to sum up
the purpose of this first historical part of the book. Its
object has been to provide a standard of measure for claims
that revolutionary changes in the basic structures of domestic and international power are in train or will happen
during the course of the twenty-first century.

The changes of the sixteenth and seventeenth centuries
in Europe were truly revolutionary in their import. The
transition of the early modern period was seen as central
by figures as diverse as Adam Smith, Karl Marx and Max
Weber. They saw it in their different ways as a transition
to capitalism. But it would be a mistake to see capitalism
as the core of the early modern transformation. At the end
of the fifteenth century 'feudal' society was already in
ruins, but capitalism in the full sense of the term existed
nowhere in Europe by 1700. Late medieval societies in
Western Europe had considerable elements of market
exchange and specialized production for trade, but these
sectors existed within an economy dominated by peasant
production. Capitalistic society based on generalized com-
modity production and exchange, in which the majority of
the population lived by wage labour and were separated
from subsistence production, first came into existence in
England in the eighteenth century and did not develop in
the rest of Western Europe until well into the nineteenth
century. If the early modern period marks a fundamental
discontinuity, what kind of transition is it, from what to
what?

The key transition is not that from feudalism to capitalism but that to the sociopolitical structures on the basis of which modern capitalistic and liberal societies could subsequently be created. These basic structures were the development and dominance of the sovereign territorial state, the development of the states system with a clear separation between internal and external policy, the concentration of warfare in the hands of states, and the development of intercontinental trade. The concentration of political power in the hands of the central state and the magnification of military force made possible by the firepower revolution created the conditions for radical social transformation towards a market economy and world trade. Centralized territorial states provided the political stability, the apparatus of legality, and the popular legitimacy necessary for generalized market systems to be created and enabled to function. They also provided the concentrated force necessary to impose wage labour and market relations on resistant populations at home and societies abroad. State power created the conditions in which market liberalism in Europe became possible. States and the system of states fostered the creation of a world trading system. States sustained exploration, conducted imperial conquests, and promoted the creation of trade relations between the different parts of the globe. Without state power long-distance trade could hardly have existed. Without the competition of states for the wealth of trade and empire, and the struggle to forestall others, the forcing of the world into a Europe-centred trading system could not have occurred.

The state/international system transformation of the early modern period created the basic structures of the modern world and these will remain, despite major changes that are likely to take place in the course of the twenty-first century. The state, the international system, and the world trading system, products of the transformations of the sixteenth and seventeenth centuries, are basic to our world and are not going to be displaced. In that sense the changes to come will take place within the framework of the truly revolutionary changes outlined in the first part of the book.

3

The Future of War

After the Cold War

The end of the Cold War has loosened the international system. It makes new kinds of wars possible and has changed the balance of military power. Russia is economically weak; its GDP is about the size of South Korea's, and its military face severe budgetary constraints.[1] Its response is likely to be a dual one, in both cases concentrating scarce resources. On the one hand, it will retain and modernize a sufficient core of its nuclear deterrent. This gives Russia the option to constrain the West and prevent intervention in its vital national interests, for example in the Caucasus. It also provides an insurance policy against China and a deterrent against a nuclear-armed Islamic power. Nuclear arms reduction enables Russia to abandon obsolete weapons and benefit from parallel US reductions. Modernizing its forces, while opposing US moves to modify the anti-ballistic missile (ABM) treaty in order to create anti-missile defences, is the best option to maximize Russia's nuclear leverage. Nuclear weapons are relatively cheap, given an initial capital expenditure. On the other hand, Russia will try to modernize its conventional forces, creating a smaller, better equipped and more motivated army to deal with threats on its borders. Currently the Russian high command is split in the priority it will give to these objectives, given scarce resources, and elements in the military are resisting modernization because it will mean force reductions and wholesale redundancies in the officer corps.

Russia will not play the same compliant role in relation to the West that it did in the early years of Yeltsin's presidency. However, it will limit its interventions and use its compliance to buy Western support. The days of the Cold War great game are over. Russia will not aid peripheral powers in the Third World against the US, but it will assert itself when necessary, as its support of Serbia in the Kosovo conflict demonstrates. Russia will remain a great power but not attempt to be a world power. That role it has ceded to the USA. During the Cold War the US sought to maximize technological advantage over the huge arsenals of the USSR. It built up a worldwide communications and intelligence system that neither Russia nor any other power could match. It developed new weapons such as cruise missiles, stealth aircraft and precision-guided munitions to increase the lethality of its forces against the huge numbers of Soviet tanks. This Cold War legacy gives it both a world reach and a technological superiority that no other state can hope to match in the foreseeable future.[2] The European powers' military forces, narrowly configured to fight the Soviets in Europe with essentially similar weapons, have been left behind. Europe is a military weakling by comparison with the US. It obtains far less effective and sophisticated forces for its military expenditures, locked up as they are in relatively small national forces. The European Union (EU) neither wants to be a rival to the US, nor will it develop a federal-level defence force. It will, however, try to create sufficient integrated national military forces to serve as a tool of common EU foreign policy in its own near abroad. In the foreseeable future the Atlantic alliance will hold. Indeed, some European capacity for autonomous action may be attractive to the USA if it is reluctant to intervene in specific crises or becomes more generally isolationist.

The end of the Cold War has left most states on their own; they can no longer attract military aid from the superpowers. This loosening of the international system reinforces the fact that states are and will continue to be ever less homogeneous in their attributes. That equality of sovereignty for all states is a fiction is clearer than ever before. During the Cold War impoverished states like Ethiopia and Somalia were given modern arsenals to fight for the worthless scrub of the Ogaden desert. Now the differences in wealth, size and governance capacity mean that there is a differences in kind between states. Some like Somalia, Sierra Leone or the Democratic Republic of the Congo have virtually ceased to exist. It is fashionable to assert that in the future, in the post-colonial and post-Cold War world, most wars will be civil wars. Social forces and economic interests will clash within the artificial borders of the colonial era, and the conflicts stoked up by the superpowers will continue to rumble on in countries like Angola. This may not be the case. States have fought one another in the last half-century – India and Pakistan, Israel and the Arab states, Iran and Iraq, Britain and Argentina – and there is no reason to suppose that such conflicts will not continue to occur. Other states are international pariahs, like Iraq, refusing to abide by international norms and threatening their neighbours.

The question is what forms of intervention are likely in such conflicts. The United Nations has proved itself indecisive and grossly incompetent in dealing with conflicts, whether within or between states. Its only real role is to provide legitimacy for the action of other powers, and, with China and Russia unlikely to comply with US policy in the Security Council, this is seldom likely to be forthcoming. The USA and its allies will, therefore, seek other justifications for intervention. States that violate international norms will be subject to sanction if the interests of the Western powers are compromised, much as delinquent or defaulting political entities were in the nineteenth century. The bombardment of Kagoshima in 1863 or the British de facto control of Egypt after 1881 should remind us that armed intervention of this kind is nothing new. One difference now is that the West has international agencies like the World Trade Organization (WTO) to enforce free trade and the International Monetary Fund to enforce financial rectitude.

New wars?

The questions about intervention are whether many more states will risk becoming pariahs because they grossly violate their citizens' human rights and whether, after Bosnia and Kosovo, Western powers will draw back and seek to avoid such engagements where possible. The danger here is to generalize from recent history, to assume that old wars are a thing of the past and that the main task for the Western powers is to equip themselves politically and militarily to fight the new wars of humanitarian intervention. The notion of new wars has produced a recent literature, much of it from radical and left-leaning commentators who see Bosnia and Kosovo as examples of just cause for military intervention. The two most influential are Michael Ignatieff and Mary Kaldor.[3]

Kaldor presents a systematic rationale for the concept of new wars and a doctrine of intervention and so it is useful to consider her case in some detail here. She argues that the new wars are a political phenomenon of the post-Cold War world that has three elements. First, that political leaders in decomposing states utilize a politics of identity, preying upon fears of sections of the population and setting them against others. Far from being a renaissance of traditional nationalism, this is a particularistic and predatory politics practised by corrupt elites to keep themselves in power and to annex wealth. Second, that violence is decentralized, war is conducted by militias and criminal bands as much as by regular forces, and war is primarily directed against citizens in the excluded group. Thirdly, the development of a globalized war economy: such failed states in the new international order have collapsed economies and their elites rely on plunder and selling raw materials on the world market to maintain their position.

There are several problems with this account. It is not easy to separate the old and new nationalisms in this way. Many earlier nationalist struggles involved deliberate ethnic cleansing and deliberate exchanges of populations afterwards. The Greek-Turkish war of 1921–2, for example, involved savage atrocities on both sides and the wholesale expulsion and transfer of populations. Many national liberation struggles were conducted by militias and bandits, especially in the Balkans. During the Greek war of independence much of the fighting was conducted by Albanian bandits on the Greek side and by irregular forces on the Turkish. The decentralization of military forces in civil wars is perfectly normal, with different localities and political forces raising their own militias: the Spanish Civil War is a good example.

Most of Kaldor's new wars involve old problems, stemming from the colonial era, or from the peace treaties after the First World War, or from the Cold War. The crisis in the former Yugoslavia has roots in the peace settlement

after 1918. This state was an artificial creation based upon
Serbia, unstable before 1939, riven by civil war during the
Second World War, and recreated by a Communist regime
after 1945. That regime was forced even under Tito to try
to contain the conflicts between the different nationalities
by federalizing the state and granting substantial autonomy
under the constitution of 1974. This slow Balkanization of
the state came apart with the collapse of the Communist
autocracy. Democratization was bound to expose the conflicting political forces in Yugoslav society. Democracy
requires a measure of political homogeneity; people have
to feel secure in being ruled by a majority party they did
not support. In the poisonous politics between the elites of
the states of the federation this was unlikely to be the case,
even without a ruthless demagogue like Slobodan Milosovic. Milosovic played upon ethnic tensions, but he did
not invent them. Swift and decisive action by the European
Union in 1991 might have stopped the civil war, but
Europe was ill suited to such decisive action and had no
military forces.

If we look at other cases, like Afghanistan, Angola and
Somalia, then we see fractured societies and weak states
torn apart by the effects of the policies of the superpowers
or of their more powerful neighbours. Forces like the
Taliban or Unita were created to destabilize the regime in
power. In such societies political power really does grow
out of the barrel of a gun, there being no strong social
order or integrated economy that can act as a check to
military force. Small bodies of armed men have a disproportionate effect. These problems are not new, moreover:
foreign intervention in these conflicts was conducted in
classic Clausewitzian terms as the continuation of policy
by other means.

Other wars are by no means as 'new' as they seem. The
Gulf War was brought on by a classic policy of interstate

aggression. The vast disparity of the outcome was only partly due to advanced technology and mainly due to a combination of poor strategy, lack of operational competence, and the low morale of the Iraqi troops. The Six Day War in 1967 involved an equally stunning victory with very disproportionate losses, and the Israelis did not have high-tech sensors or precision-guided munitions. In the Gulf War, strategic failures on Saddam Hussein's part included a failure to wait until he had an adequate stockpile of weapons of mass destruction and passively waiting in Kuwait while the Allied coalition mobilized. One might ask what the Iraqi's stock of weapons might have accomplished with the leadership of a Giap or an Ariel Sharon commanding a well-motivated army. They might have gone on to attack the Saudi capital. Saddam Hussein made the fatal miscalculation that he would not be opposed in taking Kuwait. The Iraqi army was incapable of conducting complex mobile operations; it had fought a largely static defensive war against Iran using superior firepower. The poor training and low motivation of the reservists who made up the bulk of the army were inevitable given Saddam Hussein's political system. This relied on exclusive control of political power by a tiny elite and the enforced political passivity of the mass of the population. The Gulf War would undoubtedly have led to Iraqi defeat once the USA had marshalled its forces, but it need not have been a massacre.

The case of Kosovo shows that advanced weapons will not necessarily destroy military forces effortlessly, even with overwhelming air superiority. Well-concealed and well-entrenched forces were difficult to destroy. Like Saddam Hussein, Slobodan Milosovic relied on seizing territory and defying the NATO forces to evict him. His problem was that he did not anticipate the scale of NATO bombing of civilian targets in Serbia, nor did he appreciate that NATO would contemplate a ground invasion if the air offensive failed. He did not have a sufficient degree of political support at home to sustain the campaign in Kosovo, despite popular Serb opposition to the Allied air raids. In the end it was a case of which of the two ill-considered initial strategies would unravel first, Milosovic's relying on NATO reluctance to evict him with ground forces, or the Allies' reliance on a demonstration of air power without clear options if it failed.

Kaldor's doctrine for new wars has the advantage of being clear and coherent. Her aim is a system of humanitarian intervention that would attempt to enforce cosmopolitan norms and build on 'islands of civility' within the affected countries, supported by transnational institutions. Such a process would involve 'cosmopolitan law enforcement' that 'would underpin a cosmopolitan regime'.[4] Most humanitarian military intervention has had confused objectives stemming from mixed motives. Kaldor argues that attempting to keep the peace between the conflicting parties in Bosnia, for example, was a mistake. She argues that the parties were not equally politically legitimate and that the war was not a genuine conflict of nationalities – rather it was an unequal contest between those who supported the values of civility and those who relied on a politics of fomenting hatred and enforcing exclusion.

Such a cosmopolitan policy would be disastrous. It involves picking those who are the bearers of 'civility' and favouring them politically and economically, backing this up with external force. Who will judge who are the cosmopolitans? This is a left-wing version of the Good Guys vs Bad Guys political thinking that led to disaster in Somalia. Mostly there are only different kinds of bad guys, or, rather, the good are too few or too diffuse to make a political solution based on them possible. The intelligentsia of Sarajevo was never a viable base for a political solution in Bosnia. The powers that intervene must usually deal with the powerful politicians they find in place. Even if they are bad or brutal such politicians may be persuaded or coerced into accepting some kind of solution that will end conflict, as with Clinton's coercion of the leaders at Dayton. An international politics of human rights that leaves no room for compromise, that unhesitatingly and invariably criminalizes political leaders, will find it impossible to get them to make peace.

Great Power solutions based on dealing with those who have power may be bad, but 'cosmopolitan law enforcement' will turn the greater part of the world against human rights. Sorting out the problems of the post-Cold War world is probably beyond the military capacity or the civilian political will of the Western powers. They are forced to maintain substantial garrisons in Bosnia and Kosovo for the foreseeable future. How many more such ongoing commitments will they accept? We need to evolve a doctrine that a large part of the world's states can accept, that draws on a wider set of national traditions of civility and tolerable standards of international conduct. This will not be easy, but international standards that come in a box marked 'made in America' will not be well received. This is particularly so since the history of American interventions in the last fifty years hardly shows them to be disinterested or exercised on behalf of liberty in most cases. Kaldor would undoubtedly agree with this, but the problem then for her position is that only the United States is capable of effective peace enforcement in most cases.

The West should intervene as sparingly as possible – only when there is no option and the human consequences of not intervening are sufficiently grave. Even then, action will be tempered by a calculus of proportionality, because nobody seriously advocates going to war with Russia to save the Chechens or with China to free Tibet. One must also accept that many wars and massacres cannot be remedied in time. The butchery in Rwanda would have been difficult to stop even if the powers had acted promptly. The genocide was planned and fomented by politicians, but it was not created out of nothing. The depth of intercommunal hatred led to mass participation in the massacres. It would be difficult for a foreign army to stop villagers murdering their neighbours with pangas. Britain was quite incapable of stopping savage intercommunal violence during the partition of India in 1947, for example. Intervention will remain what it has been since the nineteenth century, a mixture of realpolitik and morality. Not intervening may have some benefits, as many peoples subject to Western meddling, like the Angolans, might well point out.

The Revolution in Military Affairs

If we turn from new wars to new weapons, the central organizing theme of the discussion of post-Cold War military forces has been the 'revolution in military affairs' (RMA).[5] The debate about the RMA has been conducted at a high level in the USA, concentrating on future strategy, military organization, and the direction of weapons research and investment. Indeed, the RMA has been adopted as doctrine by the Pentagon. The central assumption of the RMA debate is that existing forces are largely obsolete. The US military is organized around platforms: planes, ships and tanks. Yet America's key assets are in intelligence gathering, communications and precision-guided weapons. The leading advocates of the RMA argue that command, control, communications and intelligence are capable of rapid development such that they will dispel the fog of war, enabling senior commanders to see the combat situation and junior ones to command complex firepower at will. Information-based strategies require a flattening of hierarchies and an integration of forces, rendering the present structures and divisions of the military less than optimal.

Martin Libicki usefully distinguishes between three phases in the RMA: Pop-up Warfare, the Mesh, and Fire-Ant Warfare.[6] The first relies on war based on stealth and sensors, relying on a protective screen for one's own forces while identifying those of the enemy and striking them with precision weapons. This is the situation now, a result of the US seeking a quality advantage over the USSR. The second relies on integrated information-collecting and processing capacities combined into a network capable of identifying enemy forces and directing economical precision weapons on to them. In this phase, relatively small forces may have very high destructive capabilities. In the third phase, sensors and weapons become fused. Platforms will have become secondary. The battlefield will be seeded with small intelligent sensors cum munitions with a capacity to function as an information-gathering network and with a high level of redundancy, so that failures can be compensated for.

If we take this division as a guide, then the Revolution in Military Affairs has hardly begun. The military situation today is rather like the 1920s. Most states, even the USA, have large obsolescent forces based on platforms such as tanks and supersonic fighters that will become increasingly vulnerable but which consume most of the available budget. This will slow down emergent technologies unless a major effort is made to divert defence expenditure into R&D in this field. The US is aware it faces this choice, but it may find it difficult to steer its forces in this direction against vested interests. Michael O'Hanlon, in the most

thorough recent review of the prospects for the RMA up
to 2020, is right to caution that many of the central
technical breakthroughs necessary to it cannot be achieved
quickly, and that some will not be attained at all.[7] Thus it
will never be possible to achieve perfect battlefield information through sensors. He concludes that the wilder
claims of its advocates should be discounted. However, his
scepticism overlooks the potential for new technologies to
interact and produce new systems like those of Libicki's
third phase. Even so, he too advocates a policy of the
cautious and scaled-down acquisition of the major new
platforms currently in development and an enhanced
emphasis on R&D.

It will take at least thirty years for the RMA to reach its
full potential. Over that time a further revolution in computing power, the development of nanotechnology (that is,
machines of molecular scale), and further developments in
robotics will make a wide variety of intelligent weapons
possible. Small but deadly submunitions, microweapons
and nanoweapons could be carried in large numbers by
cruise missiles, guided missiles or remotely piloted vehicles
(RPV).[8] Such RPV and missile systems will thus act as
'buses' for the new smart and small sensors cum weapons.
A 'Terminator' may well be possible too, that is, an
intelligent robot capable of limited autonomous action and
designed to replace conventional infantry in such difficult
and dangerous places as cities and jungles. Platforms will
tend to become transport units for such systems, although
a small core of advanced manned combat aircraft and ships
will be retained. The new transport platforms for combat
systems will probably use designs adapted from civilian
aircraft and container ships. Platforms will become less
costly, sensors will multiply and computing power will be
widely dispersed throughout the battlefield. This will mean
that very expensive and highly centralized information-

processing systems like Aegis and AWACS (airborne warning and control system) would become less central to the conduct of operations than they are for the US military now.

RMA forces would be integrated and would contain relatively low levels of personnel. They could be moved rapidly to any part of the world and they would not expose human beings involved with them to the threat of death to any great degree. This would seem to favour the United States and allow it to overcome the constraints on using ground forces.[9] A 'post-heroic' military would remove one constraint, but it would impose another, for war would cease to be a combat. Perfect information and a small risk of losses to one side would eliminate 'war' in the Clausewitzian sense; it would cease to be a moral struggle and it would cease to involve 'friction'. The use of force would become like a species of pest control. How the public would react to Terminators and nanobots ruthlessly slaying enemies is far from clear. Such systems would enable the US to overcome the aversion of the American public to casualties in foreign wars, but it would face the danger of losing the media war if such technologies led to heavy casualties among innocent civilians. The effectiveness of air power in Kosovo and Serbia was blunted by such concerns, and spectacular incidents of killing civilians by mistake came close to losing the propaganda war for the Allies and opening rifts in NATO. The odds are that even the most sophisticated sensors will not be able to look deep into buildings or to differentiate soldiers and civilians reliably.

Moreover, the technological advantage may not remain exclusively with the USA. Intelligent mines and microweapons may not be that difficult for other powers to develop. China is currently working on microweapons. Such weapons could be sown in advance and relatively rapidly to create a dense defensive web that may be difficult to penetrate. Thus whether the RMA actually favours the offence or the defence, and the advanced or the less developed powers, is difficult to determine. In the first phases, however, it will probably favour the offence and the USA. Only the US can afford to develop systems like Aegis, that enable American cruisers to track up to a hundred targets and engage several simultaneously and at long range.

Rapid changes in communications and information technology seem to make remote control wars at a considerable distance possible. Some RMA advocates imagine entirely virtual wars, with electronic warriors sending weapons into action from the USA or distant secure bases. The problem with this *Wired* magazine version of the RMA is that it concentrates too much on the computing side and too little on the link between the command post and the remotely piloted systems. Such controls still have to be based on the old-fashioned radio link, and radio waves are relatively easy to disrupt. Electromagnetic pulse (EMP) weapons and nuclear bursts in the atmosphere could reduce such a virtual army to near impotence. Satellites are currently very vulnerable too, but are crucial to the US war machine both for intelligence and for the Global Positioning System (GPS) data that smart weapons rely on to hit their targets. For RMA forces to function, these satellites will have to be duplicated and defended from attack. Space weapons, both defensive and offensive, may prove to be the most effective new truly long-distance technologies. The Bush plan for anti-ballistic missile defence is very ambitious, and has implications that go far beyond defence and could be used conventionally too.[10] RMA forces will thus have a distinct advantage only if they are supplemented and secured by a mix of different types of weapons and sensors, including some infantry. The

RMA can dramatically reduce reliance on traditional weapons, making smaller forces far more effective, but pure virtual war is needlessly risky. Even sophisticated remotely guided weapons will have to be transported near to the theatre of operations and controlled from there, not from thousands of miles away.

The other major aspect of the RMA is information warfare. As such, information warfare is not new; it has existed since the beginning of electronic communications and sensors and was widely practised in the Second World War. Examples include code breaking, signals analysis, deception using fake radio nets, and jamming sensors and guidance systems.[11] In such practices the American and British forces had a distinct advantage and this may have offset their inferior competence in ground warfare. Information war now is different in that it is capable of disabling the control systems of complex activities and not just intercepting or blocking transmissions.[12] Such warfare can be directed against either the information systems controlling military operations or those systems that control civilian activities. Hacking into military computers or the systems controlling interbank transfers, air traffic control and nuclear power stations would enable information warriors to do immense damage. Such key nodes in the system will probably be defended by adequate firewalls, given time, but a large portion of social infrastructure cannot be protected at an acceptable cost. Terrorists may then target less obvious things, like traffic control computers, or routine government–citizen interfaces, like social security. The problem for the advanced countries is that they have far more assets vulnerable to such attack than less advanced enemies. The scale of computer control is so vast that it would be difficult to get the whole civilian economy proofed against such attacks. The Fire-Ant phase of the RMA would make combat forces much less vulnerable to such disruption, since they would be based on a dispersed and loose-textured information network without highly vulnerable central nodes.

Such technical advances lead to complex asymmetries. Low-tech options are available to counter the threat of information war. One is to move rapidly into a strategic position and then go quiet. Another is to coordinate through very low-tech communications. The former is a version of the Serbian strategy in Kosovo and the latter was actively practised against elaborate arrays of US sensors by the North Vietnamese army. Quite small forces are sufficient to practise information war. The most difficult opponent for an advanced country like the USA to counter would be a very low-tech society with a small elite of cyberwarriors acting offshore.

The RMA is thus neither a recipe for effortless victory nor necessarily a panacea for continued American military superiority. The RMA will not make the battlefield transparent, but it will mean that those armed forces that seek to avoid sensors will have to give priority to concealment over either mobility or concentration to a degree unknown before. The RMA will create new more accurate and deadly weapons, allowing a more economical ratio between munitions expended and targets destroyed, but in its third phase of dispersed and decentralized systems based on weapons sensors it may well favour the defence. It may thus reverse the current tendency of high-tech weapons launched from platforms to favour mobile warfare and the offensive. The RMA may allow automated war, but to be effective that war may have to be even more brutal than now. RMA systems, even if they evolve into a Terminator, will find it harder than it is now with infantry and manned platforms to differentiate between combatants and civilians. Such a tendency to favour the defence and to automate war may increase the pressure to seek solutions to stalemate in the form of weapons of mass destruction. It might have the effect of encouraging the use of nuclear weapons to crack open sophisticated prepared defences, rather than the aim of making them unnecessary by efficient precision strikes. In particular, airburst nuclear weapons may be used to create electromagnetic pulses that destroy circuits and disrupt radio waves, thus blinding sensors.

There is unlikely to be a real equivalent of the RMA in the biological and chemical field, despite the vast advances in biological science and genetic engineering.[13] These other types of weapons of mass destruction still have even less appeal in interstate combat than nuclear weapons. They are now and will most likely remain essentially terror weapons against civilians. Events like the gassing of civilians in the town of Halabja by Saddam Hussein's air force will tend to take place against defenceless civilians and within the territories of vicious governments. Chemical weapons also have a certain deterrent effect: other states are unlikely to unleash them on a power able to make and deliver nerve gas, for example. However, their main consequence is to force armies to don cumbersome protective suits and masks and to use antidotes with unpleasant side-effects. Biological warfare may be possible if targeted diseases can be created that act for a short time on selected populations and against which one's own forces can be made immune. The problem is that most of the really effective diseases are difficult to switch off and have a nasty tendency to mutate. Only an idiot would plan to use superviruses in the hope their effects can be contained. The problem is that there is always a substantial supply of politically motivated idiots and the widespread use of the technology of genetic modification would provide them with the means to create such weapons relatively easily. We should be grateful that the Japanese sect Aum Shinrikyo tried to use Sarin nerve gas, rather than say a flu virus as deadly as that of the 1918 epidemic. Chemical and biological warfare is likely to remain sub-Clausewitzian, to be a matter of state terror against rebellious populations or terrorist attacks against cities in the West. In the latter case it will be a matter of policing and effective medical countermeasures, rather than full-scale military combat.

The causes of wars

The advanced states have currently forsworn Clausewitzian war one with another, that is, as a means of solution of interstate conflicts of interest. This is likely to persist and to include a growing number of states outside the Organisation for European Co-operation and Development (OECD).[14] Collective intervention under international legitimation and humanitarian missions are the only grounds on which such states will use force externally for the foreseeable future. Existing military forces are therefore ill-matched with actual military needs. Not only are they likely to be overtaken by the RMA, but they are ill-trained and ill-equipped for peacekeeping and humanitarian missions. Minor powers are likely to try to avoid direct military confrontation with Western powers after the experience of the Gulf War and Kosovo, but they have many other options in pursuing armed conflict. Increasingly too the enemies will not be states but other bodies like confrontational non-governmental organizations (NGOs), terrorist groups and militias. Western societies will become ever more vulnerable to terrorist attacks and will shift their efforts even further towards intelligence gathering and paramilitary policing. Such conflicts will be non-Clausewitzian, that is, they will not involve the regular armed forces of a state in a distinct state of war in pursuit of a definite policy. Such conflicts are also likely to be vicious and outside the scope of the rule of law on both sides. Western states will find it difficult to preserve limited government and a liberal society under such pressures. They are likely to respond with ever more draconian anti-terrorist laws that curtail civil rights and with extralegal retaliations against their opponents if major terrorist acts like the World Trade Center bombing become regular occurrences.

Western states will evolve more sophisticated and differentiated armed forces. High-tech warriors, the kind of well-trained and sophisticated infantry needed both to survive in an environment created by the RMA and for situations like Bosnia, and anti-terrorist forces will each have a very different ethos and will be difficult to combine in the same organization. The more radical RMA advocates claim that it ought to collapse the distinction between armies, navies and air forces leading to an integrated organization that can form pick-and-mix battle groups according to the requirements of the situation. Military constraints as well as bureaucratic inertia and political log-rolling mean this rational outcome is unlikely. The military will become more differentiated in outlook than today. Some elements may become more liberal and less combat oriented, adapted to the needs of peacekeeping and humanitarian aid. Other units, particularly the anti-terrorist forces, will tend to become more praetorian and extralegal. In the advanced states conscript armies are already a thing of the past, close to useless. Populations will have less and less military experience. Their expectations about the use of military forces will become more unrealistic and contradictory. The RMA may encourage a kind of 'remote control' bloodthirstiness, the more so as Western casualties are likely to be quite low. This will encourage leaders to

respond to terrorist outrages with precision-guided ven-
geance, like the American bombing of Libya in 1986.
Other constituencies will advocate humanitarian military
intervention. Such demilitarized populations will also produce rejectionist minorities who will either oppose the
system through violent activist groups or join the most
hard-core of the praetorian units. Civil and military values
will probably pull further apart. Already, for example, the
American military is far more conservative than US society
as a whole. This divergence will lead to the alienation of
the more combat oriented of the military and in some
circumstances might lead to a praetorian threat to political
order.[15]

The proliferation of weapons of mass destruction outside the advanced countries will be almost inevitable.
Where competing regional powers acquire nuclear weapons then the most likely outcome is a local balance of
terror, like those of the Cold War but on a smaller scale.
However, if one considers the best current example, that
between India and Pakistan, one cannot feel that it is likely
to be as robust as that between the superpowers. Pakistan
is close to being a failed state and some future leadership
may engage in a reckless adventure in Kashmir to bolster
its regime. It might respond to the threat of conventional
defeat by a nuclear ultimatum. Pakistan is only one of a
number of unstable states with or close to nuclear capabil-
ity. The possession of weapons of mass destruction by
pariah states or non-state forces may lead to greater international action, whether legitimated or covert, to destroy
such capacities. It is highly likely that terrorist groups will
carry out major nuclear, chemical or biological warfare
outrages in the advanced countries. One such action may
lead to a campaign of extermination against such groups
sanctioned by the major powers. This will resemble the

campaign against pirates in the nineteenth century but will be unlikely to be as successful.

In a world of growing inequality within and between nations it is unlikely that the poor will submit meekly. Alvin Toffler's notion of a 'revolt of the rich', in which the elites and rich regions in poor and rich countries alike seek to dump the burdens and costs of the poor, is unlikely to succeed.[16] The poor will always get into the citadels of the rich: imagine the wealthy without servants? Small numbers of terrorists and criminals can cause mayhem. The revolting rich would have no legitimacy; no revolution has succeeded on the basis of pure greed. Such anti-democratic actions would place the areas in question under threat of justified popular reprisal. The difference from past periods is that there is no unifying ideology like Communism and no 'Workers' Fatherland' to link the different revolts. Many non-state forces will engage in armed struggle both against the elites in Third World countries and against the advanced countries. Their causes will vary from deep-green environmentalism, to religious fundamentalism, to nationalist secessionism, and there will even be some socialist revolutionaries. Such groups are likely to proliferate, acting across states. They, rather than states, which are easier to face down, will be the equivalent of the 'have not' powers of the 1930s. They will have a determined will-to-power based on violent action. Some of these groups may have justified causes, others will justifiably be regarded as enemies by the whole of civilized humanity. Groups like Aum Shinrikyo are unlikely to disappear.

The absence of a unifying ideology for revolt will mean that states are less likely to intervene on an ideological basis to aid other regimes. Local elites will be left to fight their own battles, they will no longer be outposts of the

'Free World'. Social and economic inequality will continue to produce new conflicts, new 'beggars' armies' very different from the guerrilla movements of the Cold War era. One model for a new leftism in both style and content is the Zapatistas of Chiapas, using the media as a weapon and trying to spare peasant lives. Other movements will do what the revolutionaries of FARC in Colombia have done, that is, combine social struggle with taxing the profits of drug-running. Abandoned regions, like Chiapas or the North-East region of Brazil, will be breeding grounds for new rural revolts. The consequences of some of these revolts, like that in Colombia, will spill over into the cities of the advanced world in the form of drug-related crime and this may provoke armed intervention by the US.

There is little prospect of the 'clash of civilizations' propounded by Samuel Huntington.[17] The main reason is that civilizations are not homogeneous enough to group the world according to such values. Islam, for example, is by no means a uniform religion and nor are the cultures of the Islamic world more uniform than the Christian. Morocco and Java, for example, are very different places and the regimes in question have local interests. Huntington does make one major point that is worth remembering: the United States is a specific culture not a universal civilization. It cannot expect the whole world to become like it, or for others to approve to the extent that this happens. This does not mean that the West must subscribe to extreme cultural relativism or that it must passively accept any barbarity because someone claims it as part of his or her 'culture'. It does mean that we must recognize that there are other legitimate idioms in which respect for toleration, liberty and justice can be expressed. Indian democracy, for example, is a distinct and robust creation, not just a copy of Western institutions. This point rebounds against Huntington, who argues that the West should defend its particular civilizational values and interests, and face the difference of the rest. Rather, we should seek to build a common civilization between different national traditions and seek the elements of decency and respect for human worth that different idioms have in common. A brittle culture of 'universal human rights' imposed by the West is likely to fail. Only if rights are embedded in specific local political traditions and cultures can they be widely and actively defended across the globe. Human rights lawyers with armed men in tow are by no means the only or the best way to do this.

Two great unknowns

Two remaining issues stand out in the scope for future wars. I take it as axiomatic that there will be local wars between adjacent states in the less developed regions. But these will have a local and not a global impact. As mentioned, it is highly unlikely that in the near future advanced states will fight one another. This is not merely because they are liberal democracies or because they subscribe to international norms, but also because they have not had sufficient reason to. For most of this century the liberal democracies were embattled with strong enemies. In the 1930s they were confronted by the Axis powers and the USSR, and after 1947 by the Communist world. They had reason to band together. Now that democracy and the market economy are so widely accepted, liberal democracy is less of a distinguishing factor between states; rather relative wealth and governance capacity are. States with representative governments and the rule of law have fought one another: Britain and the USA in the war of 1812, Britain and Germany in 1914, and Britain and France were close to war in 1898. It is true that foreign policy in Germany was not under parliamentary control. Confronted with the extent of secret military conversations with the French, some members of the British Cabinet in August 1914 thought the same thing applied to a considerable extent to the UK as well. Given an irreconcilable clash of vital national interests, there is no inherent reason why liberal democracies may not fight each other.[18]

One reason for them to do so may occur over the next fifty years and that is environmental crisis. The evidence for global warming is now almost overwhelming.[19] The recent scientific consensus is that the world has become hotter than the best estimates of five or ten years ago supposed and that it is predicted to get hotter than allowed by earlier scientific models. The world in the second half of the twenty-first century is likely to be a far more unstable physical environment than at any time since the end of the last ice age. This will produce competing claims for vital resources: water, dry land, and energy sources. Will global warming and population growth provoke fights for resources and attempts to prevent mass migrations by force? The effects of environmental change and their timescale are still unclear. However, many scientists believe that the effects of global warming could happen rapidly, that they may be by then irreversible by human action, and that there is no proportionate relationship between causes and effects.

There is evidence that the polar ice caps are melting and that this process could accelerate rapidly, releasing far more water into the oceans than the previously cautious best estimate of a 0.5 metre rise in sea level over the coming century. If sea levels rise by up to 1 metre, then they will not just inundate low-lying coasts and islands like Bangladesh or the Maldives, but will threaten many coastal cities in the advanced world. Such changes are unlikely to be gradual but to come in unpredictable surges and to be accompanied by violent storms which reinforce their effects. Even wealthy countries will find it hard to adapt by changing settlement patterns and augmenting coastal defences. Patterns of increased rainfall and desertification are difficult to predict. Parts of southern Europe and North America could become arid. However, if the Gulf Stream were to fail as a result of the release of large amounts of cold water from the Greenland ice cap into the North Atlantic, then the climate of Britain and much of coastal northern Europe could resemble Spitzbergen.

Global warming is unlikely to be the only threat. In certain regions, such as the Middle East, water is likely to be in chronic short supply. Oil reserves are likely to be severely depleted over the next century, unless there are discoveries that match the size of the fields in Saudi Arabia. Oil prices will then rise and will drive most of the rural poor in the developing world out of the market for paraffin for cooking. This will push them to cut even further into woods and forests as sources of fuel, further reinforcing the effects of global warming. Energy crisis may be coupled with accelerating population growth. Present models assume that the world's population will stabilize after mid-century but there are reasons to doubt this. The population of China has grown far faster than the models that were developed in association with the one-child policy predicted, and currently stands at 1.3 billion as against an estimate of 1 billion.[20]

In these circumstances the advanced countries may suffer almost as much from environmental degradation as the poor ones, so much so that some of them may begin to hanker after *Lebensraum*. The prospects for concerted international action to halt global warming and ozone depletion do not look good and it may now be too late to reverse the warming process. The United States is currently quite unable under any conceivable regime to get popular support for radical measures to curtail energy consumption. Thus we should assume severe environmental effects will occur and sooner rather than later. It is highly likely that global warming will lead to masses of displaced poor people. Poor states can be easily contained militarily and mass migrations can be checked if the rich countries are ruthless enough. Such ruthlessness cannot be without political effects and a turn towards even more authoritarian regimes of surveillance and population control that will be incompatible with the kind of liberal international economy currently in existence. It implies massive investment in Soviet-style 'Iron Curtain' frontiers for example, cutting off the poorer parts of eastern Europe, and draconian controls on travel from poorer countries. What happens if the advanced countries too are facing massive environmental degradation and pressures for population movements within and between themselves? The scope for wars between nations and civil wars will increase greatly, particularly as the climate changes may be too rapid for orderly adaptation.

The state of the international economy in these circumstances is difficult to predict. One thing is fairly certain and that is that basic natural resources will become more salient than they are in the current economic system and certainly more than they are predicted to be by the prophets of the New Economy. Oil, gas, water and farmland are likely to become scarce resources. We should be worried that the only currently available technological fixes to deal with such scarcity are genetic modification to boost the supply of foodstuffs, and nuclear power for electricity generation and the desalination of water. Even if low-energy cars are developed they can at best mitigate the acceleration of the process of global warming and the depletion of oil reserves. Renewables will never substitute for current levels of fossil fuel consumption; only in combination with dramatic reductions in energy use could they become the primary energy sources. In a situation of great scarcity states will seek to control basic resources, and those states that continue to depend on popular consent will seek to ration them to ensure fairness. In these circumstances we may well see a greater emphasis on territoriality and a return to state control and planning over key sectors of the economy. This does not necessarily mean that international governance and international cooperation will decline, but it could well lead to a greater emphasis on national economies and more fraught international economic relations as states struggle to secure scarce natural resources for their populations. There is no point in sketching scary scenarios for a 'dark future' in gruesome detail. It is possible that the rate of climate change will slow down and that the most dramatic postulated effects will not occur, although this seems wishful thinking given the emerging evidence of global warming. New technologies such as fuel cells or nuclear fusion may remove the energy constraint, but the one is not yet commercially developed and the other may just be impossible. Thus there is sufficient evidence to suggest that after mid-century the world could be very different from what it is now. People may come to look at the open international economy and liberal societies in the advanced world at the beginning of this century with the same nostalgia that many in the 1930s did about the world before 1914.

The other major issue is China. China has been the subject of a mixture of boosterism and fear since the turn of the century.[21] Before 1949 American policy-makers were seduced by the idea of China as the coming power and a vast potential market. They are repeating the same beliefs and expectations today. Thus the objective of getting China to join the WTO is to regularize its place in the international economy, to contain commercial piracy, and to develop legally-enforceable property rights. Some conservative American analysts fear that China may become a great military power sometime in the middle of this century and a threat to the United States. This, however, is unlikely, given its current economic performance, unless it adopts a Soviet-style policy of favouring military industrialization at the expense of civilian growth.

China's economic recovery since 1978 has been spectacular, but this should not blind us to the continuing economic backwardness of China. It currently has a GDP smaller than Italy's with over twenty times the population. China remains a poor country with millions living on incomes of less than $300 a year. It has hundreds of millions of people living in rural poverty and a large sector of state enterprises that are economically unviable. The total of unemployed and underemployed may be as large as 200 million by 2020. China has vast regional inequalities in income, as much as 11 to 1 between different provinces on Chinese official statistics. Its elites, economic and political, are systematically corrupt and are major exporters of capital. Even after attracting impressive amounts of foreign direct investment in the 1990s, China may be a net capital exporter. It suffers from staggering levels of environmental damage. It may not be able to industrialize fully except at the price of truly appalling environmental consequences and of becoming heavily dependent on food imports. It is currently dependent on exports for manufacturing growth, since poverty holds back domestic markets even for such goods as bicycles. But it is capable of building up a substantial nuclear force and is determined to modernize its armed forces so that they can project its power beyond its borders.[22]

Thus China, if it remains united under the current regime, could pose a serious threat to its immediate neigh-

bours even if it does not fulfil the more optimistic economic predictions of Western analysts. China under
anything resembling the present regime will never become
a liberal state. It is a state capitalist autocratic regime based
on the party elite in alliance with prominent overseas
Chinese capitalists. It currently buys off the bourgeoisie
politically by letting them do what they like economically,
and seduces the poorer sections of the population with the
hope that they too will join in the economic miracle of the
coastal provinces. This may not be able to go on forever.
The communist credentials of the regime are threadbare,
and nobody believes them, but Marxist ideas serve as a
rhetoric that sustains authoritarian control. Nationalism
may be the most effective component that unites officials
with the people. It is a handy expedient directed against
the dissident nations in Western China, the Tibetans and
the Uighurs, and against Taiwan.

Currently, China rejects Western conceptions of the
international political order. It is too weak to challenge the
USA, but it is very effective at applying political pressure
on the pro-China lobby inside the US. Will China continue
to be accepted as part of the liberal trading order if it is a
member of the WTO but in practice flouts liberal trade
norms? What will the West do if China continues to
practice de facto protectionism and commercial piracy on
a large scale, to engage in systematic military and economic
espionage, and to menace Taiwan? The odds on a political
clash with an American administration less concerned to
appease China than Clinton's was must be considerable.
In a situation of economic and environmental crisis this
could get very nasty indeed. The advanced states currently
have ceased to see economic issues as grounds for conflict,
with free trade guaranteeing access to markets and raw
materials. China's systematic flouting of the rules could
provoke them to sanctions. The optimistic scenario is that

the Chinese Western-educated elite will come to see the advantages of democracy in South Korea and Taiwan, that they are unlike their Communist parents and grandparents whose experience was shaped by the civil war and Mao's regime. Even so, building any kind of fair and inclusive society and a regime that respects the rule of law will be extraordinarily difficult. Without such a project democracy is inconceivable.

This chapter is difficult to summarize since it has avoided a simple narrative of change. The best way to conclude is to divide the coming century into three. The first three decades will most likely be similar to the world of today. This will involve continued American military dominance, combined with reluctance on the part of the USA to act beyond certain limits as the world's policeman. The advanced states will continue to seek peaceful solutions to differences one with another and to seek to maintain the current liberal world trading system. Neither China nor Russia will be powerful enough to challenge US military hegemony on its own terms. Europe will remain relatively weak in its capacity to project its power beyond its own borders. Lesser powers may fight classic Clausewitzian wars. The disenfranchised will engage in non-Clausewitzian struggles and terrorism against governments and societies in both rich and poor countries.

In the middle of the century the military revolution will begin to reach maturity and the effects of environmental degradation may become sufficiently severe to alter existing economic patterns, diverting investment into countering the effects of climate change and securing natural resources. Both of these changes may weaken the advanced countries. The RMA may make possible cheap but smart weapons that favour the defence. Living standards may fall as economies shift from discretionary consumption to securing the necessities of life such as food, fuel and infrastructure. World trade may decline as economies stagnate and transport costs increase. The poorer parts of the world will suffer far worse. China is an obvious loser in a severe environmental crisis; it will have a very large population, few natural resources, and is already suffering from environmental degradation.

The last third of the century may, either, be far worse than the preceding one, an extended environmental and Malthusian crisis, or, if by some miracle the advanced countries learn to act in less self-interested ways, see an attempt to distribute resources more fairly and help to mitigate the effects of climate change and population growth. In such an extended crisis we must assume violent conflicts between nations and the probable limited use of weapons of mass destruction. The nature and outcome of such conflicts is beyond calculation.

We now turn to the likely architecture of the international system in the first part of the century.

4

The Future of the International System

Is the state in decline?

Many commentators from diverse perspectives claim that we are in a period of radical change in the basic forms of government and in the pattern of international relations. One way of assessing such claims is to return to the last major period of transition in the sixteenth and seventeenth centuries when both the international system and its member units were created. Then the exclusive territorial state became the dominant form of political organization. Now it is widely believed that the state is in serious decline and that new transnational forms of organization will substantially displace it.[1]

Such forms, if they do take over, will be very different from states. Most will be transterritorial and many will be private or at best quasi-public. If such displacement were to happen, then there are two possibilities. First, convergence on a new dominant type, much as the state replaced the variety of competing forms of organization in the earlier transition. The chief contender proposed by many for this role is the transnational corporation (TNC). In that case economic organizations would come to absorb a wide range of political functions. Second, is that a range of bodies will interact to govern across borders: international organizations, NGOs, TNCs, criminal syndicates, virtual networks, and mercenary bands. In either case this would mean that there would be no clear separation between domestic politics and international relations. The state would become at best one agency among many others. Thus there would be no international system – it would have been transformed by the decline of its member units. We would have returned to something like the pluralism outlined at the beginning of chapter 2.

In order to assess such claims we shall first consider the forces held to be driving change, then the postulated outcomes, and then consider both against the available evidence. The major forces driving change are widely held to be four: economic globalization; the new communications media and the New Economy; the decline of public welfare; and environmental crisis.

- It is conventional wisdom that economic globalization is undermining both national economies and territorial states. Markets in manufactures, services and finance have overstepped national boundaries. The monetary and fiscal policy of states is dictated by the financial markets. International competitive pressures force states to converge on a lowest common denominator in policy. The state is hollowed out and national economies vanish as transnational companies come to dominate. TNCs have no national affiliation, and where they locate is a matter of economic logic alone.
- The new communications media and the new economy they have created mean that people can trade and exchange ideas across the world rapidly and at low cost. The internet and e-commerce are reshaping both wealth and power. Both distance and scarcity cease to be constraints for many products, and people can thus

easily trade in one place and live in another. States will be undermined, but the new media will make possible entirely new virtual forms of political organization. New internet-based networks will create forms of coordination and democracy that bypass the state. Borders are irrelevant in cyberspace. Virtual communities of like-minded people will grow up across the globe, enabling people to pursue their own interests and largely opt out of territorial institutions.

- These two changes will accelerate the decline of public welfare. The successful can choose to live where they wish and yet have access to the whole globe. They will flee to tax havens and shun forms of collective consumption based on the old territorial communities of fate. They can afford private services and will reject social solidarity. Welfare states are for losers. The effect will be to implode welfare states, as those on middle incomes refuse to pick up the tax burden. States will lose powers of compulsion, taxes will be traded down to the bare minimum. Thus the territorial state in the advanced countries will have lost one of its basic justifications, the ability to compel the sharing of burdens and to provide all with adequate services.
- Lastly, the coming environmental crisis will mean that states cannot control the forces driving climate change from within their own borders. They will, either, have to accept stringent international regimes on energy use, surrendering autonomy, or, find that the consequences of unchecked climate change undermine their ability to govern.

There are several scenarios proposed for the types of social organization that will displace the territorial state. They focus, either, on the dominance of new forms of non-inclusive governance in an otherwise chaotic world, or, on the rise of forms of organization that operate above the level of the nation state. These scenarios are:

- A 'Borderless World' of liberal capitalism orchestrated by TNCs that allocate resources efficiently across the globe because they are no longer subject to market imperfections due to the intervention of national states – the most rigorous advocate of this view is the management theorist Kenichi Ohmae, but it is also accepted as a coming state of affairs by critics of global corporate dominance like David Korten.[2]

- A 'New Middle Ages', meaning the collapse of organized authority into competing plural powers acting within and beyond state boundaries – this notion has several advocates, some more and some less pessimistic in the degree of chaos and violence that they envisage. Alain Minc sees this negatively, others like Philip Cerny as 'durable disorder'.[3]

- A 'Network Society' envisaged by Manuel Castells in which power is 'no longer concentrated in institutions' but is 'diffused in global networks of wealth, power, information and images' – state governance is substantially displaced by a constellation of new forces operating on different scales, such as new cultural identities and new social movements.[4]

- 'Cosmopolitanism' which envisages a possible positive outcome in response to the relative decline of the state created by global forces, with new and inclusive forms of supranational governance emerging that will link affected interests across borders and include a democratic reform of global institutions centred on the United Nations, promoting greater fairness – the chief advocate is David Held.[5]

These scenarios are possible, not pure speculative futurology. The latter two in particular are based on impressive theorization and marshalling of evidence. Common to all is the relative decline of the state and the partial decoupling of power and territory. They envisage different forms of power, but all, except Held, predict the dominance of exclusive forms of governance. Such power may compel or persuade, but it does not seek legitimacy by including those so controlled, nor does it operate by rules that apply to all, including power holders.

Such self-interested and de facto forms of power are quite unlike the claims to serve the common interest made to legitimate representative government and thus the modern state. True TNCs would only be answerable to the bottom line, and thus to their global shareholders. Global NGOs are currently often exclusive and unaccountable, even worthy ones like Greenpeace. It offers the contract: 'give us your money, we will campaign for the environment, judge us by the results, but don't expect a vote.' Criminal syndicates use coercion only to extract resources from others with no reciprocity. Many states have been and are authoritarian, democratic governments have behaved cynically and badly. The core defence of the modern territorial state, however, has been that it is inclusive in the way no other body is, that it upholds the rule of law, and that it protects the private freedoms of the citizens who are its compulsory members.

The new forms of power could credibly make none of the above claims, cosmopolitanism excepted. Many states have been able to do so. Since the collapse of totalitarian regimes in Germany, Italy and Japan, advanced states are limited governments that purport to serve society. Thus the prospect of the state being displaced threatens most citizens with less accountable, more exclusive, and more capriciously coercive forms of power. Such governance is exercised neither by them nor on their behalf. Thus whether such a displacement of the state takes place is a matter of great concern. It is not just a change from one power structure to another, but a shift towards even less democracy and fairness than the minimum we now have in the better democratic states. Hence the need to test such scenarios against evidence.

Globalization

We begin with economic globalization. The issues here are so complex that only a summary treatment of the evidence is possible.[6] We confine ourselves to considering whether the internationalization of trade and investment is undermining the governance capacities of the nation-state in the advanced countries. Evidence of the creation of a genuine 'global' economy, rather than growing trade and financial flows between national economies, would include the following:

- Rapidly escalating trade to GDP ratios.
- A shift in output and trade to new locations as TNCs seek competitive advantage, particularly to newly industrializing countries with relatively low wages.
- The dissolution of national capital markets as global flows of foreign direct investment (FDI) replace locally sourced investment.
- The globalization of short-term financial flows that dictate real economic performance and are beyond the control of national central banks or international regulatory institutions.
- The organization of production and trade by true TNCs, that have no distinct national base and have a supranational management.

First, trade to GDP ratios for the major advanced countries are, with the exception of the USA which grew from 11.2 to 19 per cent, either not significantly greater or actually lower (as is the case with Japan and the UK) in 1995 than in 1913. In practice there is no such thing as a 'world market'. 'Free' trade is actually highly regulated by the major trading blocs and highly concentrated in the form of exchanges between the big three: the North American Free Trade Agreement (NAFTA), the EU and Japan. In 1996 this Triad, with 14.5 per cent of world population, represented 75 per cent of world GDP and 66 per cent of world export trade. The global economy is completely dominated by exchanges between the Triad and their satellites. The ratios of trade in manufactures to GDP of the Triad members are relatively low: in 1998 North America exported 2 per cent of GDP to Western Europe and 0.7 per cent to Japan, Western Europe exported 2.3 per cent to North America and 0.4 per cent to Japan, and Japan 3.3 per cent to North America and 2 per cent to Western Europe (WTO, *Annual Report*, 1999). The best summary is that the three blocs are trading extensively but at the margin, and certainly not at levels that could undermine domestic determinants of economic performance.

Second, there is little evidence of a shift of output, employment and trade from developed to less developed economies. Manufactured imports from the non-OECD countries to the OECD have grown as a percentage of OECD GDP from 0.49 per cent in 1963 to 2.3 per cent in 1992. These figures are still tiny, and could not dictate wages, employment or output in the OECD. Moreover, the balance of trade in manufactures still favoured the OECD, and in 1992 it exported 3.15 per cent of GDP to the non-OECD.

Third, FDI flows are also highly concentrated within the Triad, between 1991 and 1996 accounting for 60 per cent of world FDI. This was down from a 75 per cent share in 1980–91, but the early 1990s represented the high point of flows to emerging markets and this trend has been reversed somewhat after the Asian crisis. Capital markets remain stubbornly national and about 90 per cent or more of investment is raised at home. The share of FDI in gross fixed capital formation reinforces this point: in Japan in 1994 it was 0.1 per cent, in the USA in 1995 5.9 per cent and in Germany in 1995 1.7 per cent.

Fourth, short-term financial flows have indeed grown dramatically since the widespread ending of exchange controls in the late 1970s and early 1980s. Trading in currencies and financial instruments, at some $1.3 trillion a day, dwarfs both the funds needed to finance trade and FDI. The effect of such trading on the policies of governments in the advanced countries is arguable, however. There are two distinct issues: direct sanction by the markets of public policies they don't like; and the volatility of international financial markets acting as a trigger for crises with real domestic effects.

In the first case the markets generally move when a national policy is obviously unsustainable, as with the forced exit of the UK from the Exchange Rate Mechanism in 1992. Generally the markets are slow to react and precipitate well-established trends. Governments have never had complete autonomy in monetary and fiscal policy. The Gold Standard and the Bretton Woods system both imposed severe curbs on members, forcing them to adjust domestic policy to defend the exchange rate. In the 1950s and 1960s, for example, the UK suffered from a severe balance of payments constraint, and was repeatedly forced to restrain domestic demand. Markets and monetary systems both impose constraints on national economies, but markets do so in more haphazard and volatile ways. Despite the widespread abolition of capital controls, there remain huge differences in national policy between the advanced countries. Markets are not enforcing convergence in taxation and public policy. Thus in 1995 Sweden spent 69.4 per cent of GDP in public expenditure and Japan 34.9 per cent. Most European countries' public sectors spend about 40 to 50 per cent of GDP, whereas in the Keynesian 1960s, with apparently high national policy autonomy, they spent around 30 to 35 per cent. Indeed, in most developed societies the issue is not the retreat of the state but the growing intrusiveness of its intervention in civil society.

In the second case, that of systemic risk from the impact of failures in the international financial markets, this is an issue that needs to be taken seriously. Even insiders like George Soros have recognized this. The conversion of derivatives from a hedge against risk into a speculative instrument has significantly increased the threat of an over-exposed speculator bringing down the major financial institutions to which it is indebted. The Long Term Capital Management fiasco – in which a major hedge fund made a series of bad deals in which its liabilities threatened to exceed its assets by so much that its losses would threaten the viability of major banks – shows how real that threat is. So far the intervention of the major states and the IMF has contained the contagion effects from such crashes and also the backward linkages from emergent market crises like those in Mexico in 1994–5 and Russia in 1998. Coordinated international governance, dependent on the support of G7 and OECD governments, has so far worked. It has bailed out incautious investors, but it has also prevented impacts on real economic activity. Globalization prophets may think the state redundant, but bankers and investors in trouble do not, and demand public intervention to come to their rescue. Such governance could be greatly improved, both in the minimalist form of better crisis management, and with the extended agenda of better prudential regulation of international bank lending and the operation of hedge funds to limit incautious investment and over-exposure.

Fifth and last, there are very few true transnational companies. Most major companies are multinationals (MNCs) not TNCs. MNCs operate from a distinct national base and use subsidiary and affiliate companies to produce and trade abroad. Most MNCs are located in the Triad and these three main regions show the persistence of distinct national corporate structures and strategies.[7] Major companies with the highest level of internationalization tend to come from small highly export-oriented countries like the Netherlands, Sweden and Switzerland.[8] Typically the MNCs from the Triad sell about 60–70 per cent of their output in their home country/Triad region and have about 70–90 per cent of their assets there too. The acid test of the transnationalization of production is not the total output of companies like Ford or General Motors, since most of this is sold in North America, but the share in aggregate output of subsidiaries and affiliates. The share of such offshore production in world GDP rose from 5.2 per cent in 1982 to 6.75 per cent in 1990 and then fell back to 6 per cent in 1994. This does not show a large-scale transfer of output by major companies from their Triad bases. Thus frequently quoted figures which describe MNCs accounting for 40 per cent of global GDP are highly misleading.

There is some evidence that there are very real limits to internationalization, let alone globalization. The current wave of international mergers and acquisitions is probably nearing its end. Its benefits to companies, rather than to the investment bankers, are dubious in many cases and usually amount not to transnationalization but to the control of one national company by another, as with the mergers of Chrysler and Daimler-Benz or Mannesman and Vodafone. Trade to GDP ratios between the advanced countries may be approaching feasible limits. Evidence shows that borders do have a significant effect on trade.[9] Thus Canada, despite membership of NAFTA, has a level of interprovincial trade much larger than might be expected taking locational factors into account, and correspondingly cross-border trade with the US is less. Similar effects can be observed in Europe. Thus the boost to growth from the European single market was more modest than that predicted in the official EU Checcini report, which predicted major gains from integration. Further liberalization of merchandise trade may lead to no more than modest growth, hence the push by interested parties, like US investment bankers, to open up investment and to liberalize trade in services. The WTO is a rules-based organization created by treaty; it relies on the agreement of states to evolve its rules. Its rules oblige states not to discriminate, but they still allow tariffs and quotas. It polices fair rules not free trade. Hence the major trading blocs still have extensive obstacles to trade, particularly barriers to trade from developing countries.

The issue is thus not why are transnational companies so powerful but why are there so few of them? Far from growing out of and supplanting the major states, TNCs are mostly from small states, and continue to have a close relationship with them, or from certain sectors, like oil. Even then few of these are true transnationals, just nationally based companies with high ratios of export sales and large numbers of employees in foreign subsidiaries.

Companies remain nationally based for many reasons. The first is that they benefit from national systems of production and innovation. They also benefit from a distinct management culture, a store of rules and tacit knowledge which cuts training and supervision costs. A national location also helps companies to maintain a corporate identity – brands are mostly based on specific cultural associations. The increasing importance of international trade for companies also paradoxically gives greater saliency to national location. Contracts, property rights and patents are more securely protected by the legal systems of the major advanced countries. The USA is a fierce defender of the commercial and intellectual property rights of national companies. Even the widespread reception of 'Anglo-Saxon' legal standards and the growth of private commercial arbitration indicate that it is some states, companies and legal cultures that benefit more than others. The 'globalization of law' thus actually reinforces the power of some states. It also gives a distinct advantage to the big Anglo-American accountancy, consultancy, and law firms. Rights enforced in the US courts and approval by US regulatory agencies are recognized worldwide.

There are inherent disadvantages in true transnational companies too. They would need some supranational cultural cement to ensure commonality and loyalty. The advantage of national location for most senior executives is that they have access to job markets; most Anglo-Saxon senior executives expect to move frequently to further their careers. However, most real international organizations have been non-commercial, like the Catholic Church or Amnesty, and commerce seems unlikely to provide an adequate focus for lifetime loyalty. If major states declined radically in governance capacity, companies would have to provide their own enforcement infrastructure. This would be a 'bad buy', increasing costs as against companies still protected by states. States by contrast are a 'good buy', in particular since it is the customers who fork out most of the cost in taxes. Hendrik Spruyt (whom we discussed in chapter 2) may be wrong about this logic operating effectively in the Middle Ages, but the advantages for companies of physical and legal protection by territorial states are evident today. A world secured by the major states is cheaper and more effective for companies than one in which they have to secure their own trading environment in a world made chaotic by the decline of the state.

Major multinational companies are thus not suprisingly clustered in the major states. Of the 500 largest MNCs, 441 are located in the Triad and only 16 outside the OECD, most of the latter being energy companies.[10] To be useful to companies, political power has to be territorial, located where their major activities are, and capable of acting internationally – such power is of course a state. Far from leading companies to displace states, an open international economy leads to symbiosis with them. Internationalization has tended to reinforce the state rather than undermine it, at least in the major powers.

The new economy and e-democracy

The issue of the new communications media involves two distinct dimensions: first, e-commerce and the delocalization of business; and second, the rise of dotcom democracy. The first thing to note is that the internet is in no sense global. The UN's *Human Development Report 1999* points out: 'in mid-1998 industrial countries – home to less than 15 per cent of people – had 88 per cent of internet users'.[11] Sub-Saharan Africa and most of South Asia are internet deserts. Mobile phones and computers could transform the lives of the poorest, linking them with sources of information they could not otherwise access. The rural poor are most in need of the abolition of distance through the net, and the marginal cost of a phone call is close to zero.

That is not the point of the internet. Apart from a few

aid programmes to bring communications to the poor, and the public sector in the advanced countries, the purpose of the net is to make money. Currently, this is proving tougher than anyone expected and if this situation persists it will slow down investment and the development of the internet. E-businesses are struggling in the OECD countries as market growth fails to meet early expectations. In the USA there are signs that ownership of personal computers and internet use have plateaued for the time being. The potential of the new digital services is huge, but difficult to exploit. The problem lies in the paradox between the ease of access to online information and the need to make money selling it. Digitalized information comes close to abolishing scarcity and distance. Millions of copies can be made of digitally stored information at almost zero cost and multiple users do not crowd one another out. Information is easy to copy and transmit. This is a commercial nightmare since it brings information close to being a public good. To commercialize it technical barriers to access and copying have to be erected that reduce the utility of the new media, forcing people to pay for use, and control over access has to be reinforced through intellectual property rights. Hence Internet Service Providers (ISPs) and e-commerce companies, once fierce economic liberals, have become eager defenders of law. For this they need the state both domestically and as an international champion. Thus the rapprochement between the information technology industry and the US government.[12]

Digitalized goods and services are one aspect, while the other is to use the internet as a tool to market physical goods, whether directly to consumers or business to business. The key constraints here are that goods need to be capable of standardized description and quality – so that certain commodities like books, CDs and airline tickets have proved successful, while others have not – and that products ordered online need to be backed up by efficient fulfilment services. They are therefore subject to most of the limitations of the old economy. Amazon is not so different from a mail order pioneer like Sears. Companies thus cannot dispense with physical infrastructure and territorial limitations in this sector of e-commerce.

New economy companies are subject to other spatial constraints too. In theory some of them could locate anywhere, but they don't, they cluster with other companies of the same kind. Companies need to stick close to skilled labour markets; marketable workers will want to stay close to other firms where they have career options. There are real locational advantages in being part of the digital equivalent of an industrial district. To be isolated is to miss out on key localized services, on the tacit knowledge essential in a rapidly evolving industry, and on specialized venture capital. The technology makes wide dispersion possible but firms cluster in Silicon Valley, Seattle and outside Boston. The same phenomenon was observed in the 1980s in the financial markets when new technology allowed them to trade rapidly in large volumes anywhere in the world. Such markets clustered in the old financial centres of London, New York and Tokyo.

The New Economy will not end geography, nor will it do more than add a new sector and new options to the 'old' economy. This was already dominated by the service sector and communications, and was thus knowledge based. E-commerce is unlikely to get big enough in the near future to undermine sales taxes, let alone state revenues. Even if it does make some inroads, the continued territorial location of the New Economy and its customers will merely stimulate the fiscal ingenuity of states, which may switch to turnover or property taxes.

Will the net transform politics? Some argue that it

already has. The coup against Gorbachev was frustrated in part through the small Russian computer network. The coalition against the Multilateral Agreement on Investment (MAI) and mobilization against the WTO meeting in Seattle were largely organized over the net. This is surely evidence of the inability of states to control information flows and that new forms of organization are emerging outside formal political structures.

One must be careful. The internet is a decentralized system and thus technically hard to censor, but states *could* control information if they decided to be draconian enough to force firms into compliance. The police and intelligence services in the UK, USA and Russia would all like complete storage of all e-mails and keys to all encryption programmes. Big Brother is as possible an outcome of the new technologies as anarchy in cyberspace. It is unlikely to happen, for several reasons: because most governments are not interested in the ideological conformity of their populations; because it is futile, as the messages of criminals are likely to get lost in the noise if the whole traffic is regularly monitored; and because most states are scared of harming the competitiveness of their own 'e' firms with excessive regulation.

As for dotcom democracy, it does allow groups to organize in new ways and otherwise diffuse constituencies to constellate into effective groups. It thus overcomes some of the limitations on collective action that had become constraints on the old politics, and that is generally all to the good. It may thus revitalize politics and help to keep the conventional political parties on their toes. What it will not do is to displace territorially based forms of democracy. Territorial democracy, even if voting and canvassing come to be mainly conducted online, provides a means of selecting governments and giving them legitimacy. This is the reason why representative democracy remains the core of modern democratic politics; it controls access to power in territorial states. It is also why all other democratic or representative mechanisms – corporatist structures based on functional representation, associative democracy, deliberative democracy, etc. – have never been more than supplements. Adult suffrage and territorial constituencies are inclusive in a way that other mechanisms are not – they do not involve an explicit political choice as to what interests are represented or not. If states remain salient, then representative democracy will remain a necessary concomitant of those with fully legitimate regimes.

A global dotcom democracy implies self-governing communities that are voluntary and, therefore, exclusive. There is nothing intrinsically wrong with that, and the author has advocated the reform of democratic governance using self-governing voluntary associations. Such forms of organization provide new resources for campaigning to influence the policy of states and international organizations, and they can provide links for cross-border virtual communities. However, they lack the capacity to supplant rather than supplement territorial governments precisely *because* they are virtual. Thus they rely either on voluntary compliance or on persuading members to take action against local defaulters. It is difficult for the latter form of enforcement to be rule-bound. Since virtual communities do not include all, they can govern only their members and have no legitimacy to govern all. Hence they will tend to lose out if they clash with legitimate territorial governments. Such virtual communities are no better or wiser than national governments: everyone from the Red Cross to the militias in the US uses the internet. The protests against global capitalism in Seattle and Prague dramatize the problems of international governance, but they cannot solve them. They are positive to the degree that they shake up the complacent leaders inside the conference centres, but no more than that. They are unstable coalitions of protest based on diverse interests and without coherent alternatives. The internet is not an alternative to the state, and most people will carry on using the net not to make political contact with strangers but for business, hobbies, and to e-mail friends and family.

The end of welfare?

The issue of the decline of publicly funded services has been used to raise the prospect of societies rigidly segregated between rich and poor, in which the former escape from fiscal obligations and the latter are unable to bear the costs of modern welfare states. This threat combines the notion of 'winner takes all' markets with the possibility of spatial segregation, where the rich earn incomes in one place and live and are taxed in another. Elements of this scenario do exist in the USA at local level. The differential between the top and the rest has increased markedly since the 1970s; thus chief executives of top companies now earn some seventy-five times more than shopfloor workers. Across the USA exclusive suburbs and towns exist where the rich contribute to good services for themselves and property prices exclude the poor.

The question is whether such trends might be generalized into a dystopian 'Blade Runner' society in the advanced countries, in which a wealthy elite lives a completely separate life from an impoverished and excluded mass. In very unequal developing countries like Brazil mass poverty limits growth, and hence confines wealth to a small elite. Western cities are not like São Paulo, and will not become so. The main reason is that the macroeconomics of the dystopia stink. Modern advanced capitalism requires high mass consumption and that depends on mass prosperity to ensure effective demand. The distinctive feature of the USA is not so much the rich as mass affluence, from which about 25 per cent of the population are excluded. Not only have top incomes grown, but the whole managerial and supervisory class has grown hugely from about 12 per cent of the labour force in 1948 to nearly 20 per cent in the early 1980s.[13] America's imperfect welfare state is not a new thing. Low social solidarity means that the affluent masses support welfare programmes that benefit themselves, such as Social Security and Medicare, but not those for single mothers or the long-term unemployed.

In continental Europe the situation is different: inequality is generally less, social solidarity is higher, and benefits are more inclusive. Yet European welfare states have never been financed mainly by transfers from the rich, but by redistribution within the mass of the employed population, from young to old, healthy to sick, and employed to unemployed. Welfare states are under pressure in Europe but from sources largely unconnected with globalization and 'winner takes all' markets, such as persistent unemployment, high rates of family break-up, an ageing population, and rising costs of healthcare. Welfare states will have to adapt to survive, but the evidence is that they can do so. Thus in the mid-1980s the Netherlands appeared to be a stagnant economy, with unsustainable levels of unemployment and welfare dependency. In the early 1990s governments engaged in an impressive programme of economic and welfare reform, which increased employment and growth while maintaining relatively generous benefits. In the mid-1990s Sweden was seen by economic liberal critics as a paradigm case of why an extensive welfare state could not survive the pressures of global competition. Sweden has weathered the conjunctural crisis and has recovered, and despite cuts offers generous benefits by international standards.[14]

The USA, continental Europe, and Japan continue to have very different social structures and welfare systems. There is no sign that they will converge on a minimalist welfare state. States will continue to be attractive to citizens because of the services they provide.

Environmental crisis

Climate change is a real threat to the affluent life that the advanced countries have enjoyed and a menace to poorer nations. Certainly, a tough treaty regime and concerted action by states might prevent future levels of energy consumption reinforcing changes that are far advanced. States would have to comply with external norms, but this would be nothing new. This is unlikely to happen. In the circumstances of unchecked climate change, territorial states with inclusive policies that attempt to protect all citizens will become more rather than less necessary. States will use public funds to acquire scarce resources and will ration them, and they will use public action to cope with the direct physical consequences, such as flood and drought.

If one accepts the above evidence then we are not in a period of transition. The territorial state, and thus the international system, will both survive, and, indeed, may be reinforced. The first three scenarios outlined on p. 113 are thus improbable; we shall return to global democracy later. One further reason why we cannot expect a transition to a New Middle Ages, to a pluralist disorder of competing governance, is because the economic foundations of modern societies are entirely different. Medieval society could tolerate competing governance because it was based on localized subsistence production. A low division of labour permits limited coordination and can cope with periodic crises of authority. Modern extended divisions of labour both national and international depend on a high level of consistency in the behaviour of both governing agencies and other social actors. Reduce the certainty that remote actors will meet expectations, and trade will begin to unravel and with it output and growth. Complex societies need a division of labour in governance that matches that in the economy. 'Gaps' in governance, like tax havens and offshore banking for hot money, threaten the whole edifice, as do conflicting competences of agencies. The present division of labour in governance is far from perfect, but anything less would lead to economic instability and that would promote political support from business and citizens for public action to restore coordination. 'Durable' disorder is problematic, though this does not mean that a serious collapse of international governance and with it economic stability is impossible. We should remember that the chaos of the first half of the twentieth century came not from non-state actors undermining governments but from strong states trying to dominate. The First World War and the Great Crash weakened the international economy and interstate cooperation. These catastrophic events led, however, neither to pluralistic chaos nor weak states, but to the conflict of states seeking to monopolize control both domestically and internationally.

The future of the state and the international system

The international system will continue well into this century. It has three foundations: a world economy centred on the major Triad regions, with high levels of trade and investment between the distinct national economies; a population of nation-states, differing in power and legitimacy, the most powerful of which are the principal actors across national frontiers; and a system of functionally specific agencies of supranational governance, sustained by the principal nation-states.

The continued salience of the state does not mean a diminishing role for supranational governance. Interdependence between nations will continue to grow in density and complexity. A division of labour in governance has developed because certain issues can only be handled at the supranational level, while others are best handled by governments – regional, quasi-public and private – subsidiary to the nation-state. Given the complexity of many issues, from setting banking rules to overseeing atomic safety, intergovernmental relations and treaty-based norms are no longer enough; there must be coordination and regulation by standing agencies. Such bodies have grown significantly in number since 1945.

It would be a mistake, however, to conclude that such agencies are growing at the *expense* of states, nor should we infer from a complex division of labour that the state has become merely one player among many. The nation-state is different from other governing powers in two respects: it is exclusively territorial, and it defines citizenship. Extended international governance requires the sovereign territorial state in order to function. Why? Because the state is the ultimate source of responsibility for a given territory. It can be held to account internationally for action within its borders in a way that no functionally specific body or network can. States matter because they are bearers of liabilities, but they also provide the enforcement crucial to the maintenance of international norms. States are the providers of military force necessary to enforce international law, especially as the principal and most difficult defaulters are other states. States do this more efficiently and with less of a threat to liberty than any other form of governance. States have a monopoly of the means of violence only within their own borders, and thus they constrain and limit each other's use of force. As Kant realized, an effective supranational monopoly of military force would become a tyranny.

States are not only rule enforcers, they are also rule followers. Without a population of states accustomed to abide by the rule of law at home, international law could not function. International law is generally upheld, but because states have autonomy, even major democratic states sometimes refuse to comply with international norms and judgments. The case of the USA is obvious. The point, however, is not that rules are sometimes flouted, but that limited governments that act lawfully internally are likely to honour the international commitments they have made.

International bodies and commitments established by treaty, like the WTO, are able to work because states tend to be consistent actors through time. States use their powers of autonomous action to make commitments, but then tend to limit them by abiding with the results. States, if they are stable and democratic, can legitimately speak for the citizens of that territory. The state is ultimately the exclusive source of public commitments across its borders. The commitments that democratic states make are reliable internationally, because it is highly probable that successor administrations will honour previous treaty obligations.

States are the main vehicles of political accountability, and they are the principal means whereby international agencies can be supervised. If states are democratic and conform to the rule of law, then they have primary legitimacy both internally and externally. Thus they not only credibly represent national populations, but also have the capacity to challenge other states and international agencies on the basis of this popular endorsement. NGOs may criticise supranational bodies and focus attention on issues, but they have little inherent legitimacy. They represent only themselves and their own members. States, because they are themselves accountable and participate in the constitution of such bodies, have both the credibility and the standing to hold international agencies to account. States also, by endorsing the rules of operation and the actions of such bodies, donate a secondary legitimacy to international agencies. This donated legitimacy enables those agencies to function, especially when they confront individual states. Thus the IMF can act, not just because governments are desperate for a loan, but because the conditionality that it imposes will be underwritten by the major states that provide the bulk of its funds. Critics of the IMF have to start from the fact that its policy is unchallenged by the members of the G7 because they share its policy, not because they are powerless to hold it to account.

States remain the primary locus of identification and solidarity for the majority of their citizens. This is in spite of, or maybe because of, the growing ethnic and cultural diversity in most of the advanced countries. Supranational inclusive bodies like the EU or UN are obviously incapable of supplanting such national loyalty. Most other bodies tend to be functionally specific and thus can make only partial demands on the loyalty of their members. International 'civil society' is made up of such bodies. The state is not challenged by conflicting political obligations in the way it was during the Reformation, or even in the 1930s. Nobody now thinks of the UN as idealists once did of the League of Nations, as a potential world government.

States continue to thrive, despite international governance, because the factors outlined above operate to favour exclusive territorial governments. The forces working to favour the state over other agencies have changed since the seventeenth century, but a logic still operates in favour of territoriality. International governance would be weaker, less durable and less accountable to the extent that it is not founded on a population of strong democratic states.

States are not just part of the division of labour in governance, major democratic states are the key nodes that tie the whole network together. States manage the constitutional ordering between national and supranational, national and subsidiary, public and private governments. States donate sovereignty upwards and downwards, to give governance capacity to other bodies. States, as the main sources of law and accountability, are the only bodies that can do this across the full range of governance, from town hall to World Bank. The basic core of the traditional conception of sovereignty has not been displaced, that is, that there is no territory without an exclusive ruler and that effective rule will eventually be recognized by other states. Sovereignty has never been absolute, despite the definitions of lawyers, nor have states ever been capable of controlling everything within their borders. The key feature of modern state sovereignty is the capacity to manage the interactions of different governing bodies and to distribute competences between different levels of governance.

The old Bodinian conception of sovereignty as finite and inalienable made sense in a context where the state was appropriating powers from other bodies within its territory and seeking to exclude external claims to its subjects' loyalty. The apparent paradox now is that the state is possessed of far greater governance capacity, it provides vastly more public services and spends three times the share of national income it did before 1914, and yet it shares governance with bodies within and without in a way it did not before. The paradox is real only if we still view sovereignty as a zero-sum game, that any exercise of power by another agency must be at the expense of the state. This is to see governance capacity and the tasks of government as fixed quanta.

However, supranational governance does not necessarily detract from the governance capacity of states. International governance stabilizes aspects of the states' environment, for example, by containing financial crises, and by enabling commerce to enjoy common standards across borders. This makes the conditions for domestic policy more stable, and allows government to be more extensive and effective. Thus the EU, in promoting cooperation rather than conflict, and in fostering inter-European trade, has made national governments richer and able to divert their energies to public services. Europe's states have forgone the options of war, capital controls, and tariffs, but it would be difficult to argue that they are weaker as a result. Sovereignty is no longer primarily the power to exclude, but acts across borders in the collaboration of states in governance and in their donation of capacity by treaty to international bodies.

The two essential foundations of the current system are the open international economy and the nation-state. Our historical survey has shown us that free trade, rather than generalized protectionism, is the only basis for international interdependence that has proved relatively durable. We have also seen that openness requires a sizeable population of liberal states willing to uphold it. There are two main threats to the continuance of this system. One is when states engage in conflict primarily for balance of power reasons, as in 1914. The other is when the operation of the system leads to instability and to inequality between nations that ultimately fosters conflict between states, as in the 'twenty years' crisis' after 1918. As E. H. Carr recognized, Western liberals before 1914 and after 1918 could not see the extent to which the system favoured the 'have' powers and how the rules of the game acted to the benefit of these founding powers.[15] This inherent inequality is now the primary source of possible threats to the international economic system and thus in the long term to peaceful relations between states. There are enormous and growing differences in wealth and governance capacity between states. There is growing economic inequality between peoples. The current economic regime, founded under American hegemony in 1945, systematically favours the rich nations and the Triad in particular. The difference between now and the 1930s is that the 'have not' nations are economically and militarily weak.

Is the current international system viable and durable? The real threat comes not from the decline of the state, but from the ossification of the system and the perpetuation of exclusive advantage to a few powers. Whether change takes place depends on new powers emerging to challenge the beneficiaries of the present system and their dominance of its institutions. This challenge would be nothing like the actions of the revanchist powers in the 1930s, but Western economic liberals are complacent if they think it will not happen at all.

How much convergence?

Most states are marginal players in the international system; they lack the economic, military and organizational resources to assert themselves. Thus the international agencies that are effective, in their own terms at least, such as the IMF, operate at the behest of the G7. Agencies that are accountable to all states, like those of the UN, tend to be underfunded and ineffective. States will continue to differ vastly in power. The failure of free-market development strategies, as evidenced by the Asian crisis, and the closing off of the option of state-sponsored strategies of 'forced draught' industrialization behind tariff walls, like those that propelled Japan and South Korea to developed status, mean that relatively few poor countries will join the club of industrialized nations.

The problem that many radical critics see with the present international system is actually the reverse of 'globalization', and this is the spread of American economic power, institutions and ideas throughout the world – often treated as meaning the same as globalization. Will the bulk of the world in fact converge on American economic models, giving the US a continuing competitive advantage? Such inherent advantage built into the world economic system would persist, even if the US became more politically isolationist.

This is difficult to assess. An open trading system needs to converge on some set of common norms.[16] Large flows of FDI create the need for some convergence in standards of accounting and corporate governance. Currently trade rules, commercial law, accounting standards and company structures are being defined by 'Anglo-Saxon' institutions and practices. The danger is that this will lock in their rules of the game to the detriment of other societies. For example, this will empower the big Anglo-American accountancy, consultancy, and law firms, leading to control by a few multinational giants. US-style capital markets and companies driven by shareholder value are not the best route to economic development for most countries. World economic development does not just need competition between firms in product markets, but also competition between types of institutions and practices. Without such alternatives there will not be distinct routes to competitive advantage, or the possibility of competition, learning and cross-fertilization between different national styles of capitalism. Thus after 1945 the Japanese learned greatly from America, and profited from technology transfer, and in the 1980s American firms learnt in the reverse direction. The danger now is not cross-fertilization but the creation of an institutional monoculture. Thus 'Anglo-Saxon' institutional and intellectual hegemony will not only favour the dominant economic species, but would threaten economic evolution driven by competition between diverse institutions.[17]

The odds are that this tendency to dominance will be resisted and challenged. A recession in the US will encourage the French, Germans and Japanese to persist with their own economic and social institutions. If diversity persists, then economic practices will not become uniform, and multinational companies will have to continue their current practice of adapting to distinct national institutional settings. The principal reason why diversity will survive is that state and business elites will not converge. Thus the creation of a true international 'technocracy' will be inhibited. Such a cosmopolitan managerial class, public and private, with more interests in common with each other than with those of people in their countries of origin, would pose a real threat to national governance. Major states would remain powerful but that power would be used on behalf of a supranational elite. This is the most real threat of all the globalization fears. The makings of this class can be seen in business class lounges and five-star hotels across the world.

Already radical NGOs are a counterweight to such a technocracy, and they campaign internationally against the consolidation of its interests. More significant are the divergent state elites within the G7, with France and Japan sharing the 'Anglo-Saxon' view least. Thus French intellectual opposition was crucial in blocking the MAI. The most powerful non-Western countries such as China, India and Russia are beginning to speak with alternative voices in international bodies. Such states have large intelligentsias capable of evolving alternative discourses and challenging the American dominance of economic argument. A bloc of such nations is already forming in the WTO and is building alliances of less developed nations to argue for a different regime of international trade.

If international governance does become somewhat more polycentric, it will also become more conflictual. Some international bodies are more open to pressure than others. The IMF is in practice a plutocracy, while the WTO is in theory an equal partnership of states. International economic liberalism will either have to be redefined to accommodate greater institutional pluralism and fairness in outcomes, or it will be challenged with increasing vigour by states outside the charmed circle of the OECD. Less developed countries want a fairer deal in trade. Many states will resist anything resembling the MAI, which would have threatened public services and allowed companies the means to strike down democratic public policies. If the economic liberals attempt to go much further they will incite a backlash. The result will be a war of attrition by negotiation in international institutions. The poor will not be able to transform the system, but the rich will be unable fully to follow the economic liberal agenda.

The Triad's current stance, and particularly that of the USA, is only weakly legitimate internationally as it is so obviously self-interested. In both trade and climate change negotiations the Triad powers are not willing to surrender their own advantages in favour of effective regulatory regimes that might be sustainable in the long term. The EU is somewhat more open, but the position of the USA is intransigent. It wants asymmetrical benefits from trade and the right to consume as much energy as it pleases. It ensured that the Kyoto protocols on CO_2 emissions would be weak and torpedoed the negotiations at The Hague. One should not see an element of conflict in international institutions as a bad thing – it will mean greater pluralism as more distinctive voices are heard, not just those of the G7. Conflicts will give greater salience to such international issues and thus focus the attention of concerned publics in the developed countries. Hence the value of campaigns like Jubilee 2000, which shamed the rich countries on debt relief. The odds on complete convergence leading to total American institutional hegemony are remote, but equally the reality of Western economic dominance will not be overthrown.

How much democracy?

There are more countries that are formally democratic today than at any time. Even if the majority of states remain undemocratic or only partially democratic, the genuine democracies face no serious international challenge by authoritarian regimes. This is no cause for complacency. It cannot be argued that the effective international institutions are democratic, in the sense that the representatives of the majority of the world's population have the decisive say in them. Equally, it is difficult to argue that most of the mature democracies are in good health, given the current levels of political cynicism, voter abstention, and corruption.

David Held has rightly and cogently raised the issue of why should democracy stop at the boundaries of the nation-state?[18] Many issues have overstepped its borders and require international regulation, but we have no way of including all those whose interests are affected in decisions, or means of making international institutions accountable to the majority of the world's people. He has proposed a response in the form of 'cosmopolitan democracy', institutions of greater international inclusiveness and fairness organized chiefly through the UN.

It would be difficult to deny the need to tackle cross-border issues, like climate change, or the legitimacy of the goals of greater fairness and inclusiveness. The chief problem with cosmopolitan democracy is also the main reason why it is proposed, global inequality. In 1997 the share of world GDP between countries was:

> Richest 20% of countries – 86% of world GDP
> Middle 60% of countries – 13% of world GDP
> Poorest 20% of countries – 1% of world GDP.[19]

This distribution is unlikely to improve; inequalities have widened as the richest pull away from the poorest. The rich countries trade ever more intensively with each other, and the poorest have little place in the world trading system. World poverty, however, is not just relative. To the bottom 20 per cent it means the threat of hunger, disease and early death for hundreds of millions of people.

The problem is that democracy requires a measure of homogeneity in the demos, and differences of this order remain impossible to assimilate within inclusive and democratic international institutions. Western publics are unwilling to share their wealth – public aid and private charity remain paltry. Without a major transfer of resources, inclusiveness is inconceivable. The world is not going to even up spontaneously, as economic liberals believe. The citizens of wealthy countries, even domestically solidaristic ones, are never going to allow the majority decisions of supranational institutions to redistribute their national income. Imagine the population of India having the decisive say in what to do with the GDP of Germany?

States continue to have a rationale because they are locally inclusive organizations. Unfortunately international governance is effective and accountable to the extent that it is exclusive. The rich nations control and pay for the key institutions. Inclusive institutions like the UN are not merely ineffective, they are also only weakly legitimate. Majority resolutions in the UN General Assembly, where they conflict with the interests of Western states, have little credibility, and not merely because the states in question are too weak to give effect to their policies. Even if its constitutional position in the UN were strengthened, the General Assembly could never be the focus of legitimate decisions on world governance. A majority made up of states most of which are themselves undemocratic or at best only nominally so will have little force with the mature democracies. Thus we face the uncomfortable paradox that institutions of international governance are accountable and legitimate to the developed democracies on the condition that they are undemocratic on a world scale.

Equally, of course, such governance by and for the rich is problematic. It is currently either for the developed world alone or imposed on the poor and weak. This limits its scope, and therefore effectiveness, because it limits its wider legitimacy. Self-interest means that certain vital problems have to be off the agenda, because to tackle them would involve extended cooperation between rich and poor states. Unless such exclusive Western-controlled institutions begin to work towards more than nominally inclusive goals, they will not be accepted as governing fairly by the rest of the world. This needs to go well beyond creating a 'user friendly' image, as with the World Bank. This change can only come if an alternative politics of development is accepted by publics within the developed states. Greater polycentricity and greater conflict within international institutions may or may not mobilize opinion in the mature democracies in favour of more generous goals. It could also produce a backlash by the 'haves'.

National democratic effectiveness and international democratic fairness and accountability are linked. Greater inequality within the advanced nations weakens political participation. At its worst democratic politics, as in the USA, comes to resemble a plutocracy: a government of the rich, chosen by a minority of citizens, and for the rich and well-to-do. Nations with a more egalitarian distribution of income tend to be both the most domestically inclusive and the most internationally concerned, for example the Netherlands and the Nordic countries. Without an active democratic public life, state elites will be under little domestic pressure on their external policies or to hold supranational bodies to account. The OECD countries can have real influence in such bodies, but most of the time public indifference means that control is seldom exercised outside narrow technical agendas.

These contradictions are difficult to resolve. There is little prospect of greater cosmopolitanism, even in the form of well-meaning but non-inclusive action by significant numbers of the rich states. There is no evidence that the major powers can cooperate in promoting real inclusion. The most they have been able to achieve is limited debt relief and poverty reduction strategies within a wider economic liberal framework that continues to reproduce international inequality. The Bush presidency is even less likely to cooperate. The USA has de facto veto power in the major institutions and can wreck or dilute any treaty regime.

Even if this were not so, there are also intrinsic problems with democratic accountability in more extensive and inclusive global governance.[20] The current international institutions are answerable to some states, but how answerable would reformed institutions be to the many? How can one construct equitable decision procedures for quasi-polities of this kind, that are functionally specific and whose membership is made up of states? The more inclusive and numerous the active membership, the less say any one state has, thus reducing the current effective voice of the wealthy states but not necessarily increasing the real power of the enlarged membership. How could voting be made fair between such states if real decisions are to be made? Giving voting power by population, according to contributions, or on a one state one vote basis are all equally unsatisfactory in different ways. In the absence of a real majority vote, decisions will remain less than fully legitimate on the central criterion of democracy – but were such majority decisions to be possible they might still alienate powerful minorities. These difficulties with decision procedures may seriously damage the most developed supranational body, the EU, as it becomes larger and less homogeneous expanding eastwards.

It is unlikely that such problems could be resolved by a strong secretariat playing the role of 'guardian'. Because compliance and effective implementation of decisions will remain with states, dissenters have real power to undermine collective decisions. A strongly centralized institution based on the majoritarian principle and with means of enforcement would become a quasi-state, with states as the indirect electors, and this would be unacceptable to most democratic publics in the different nations. An institution that avoided this problem by working through consensus or with veto powers based on qualified majorities would have little capacity for effective decision-making. Such dilemmas of democratic accountability will exist whatever policies the rich countries adopt, or however effective the non-OECD countries are at pushing counteragendas. Political theory and institutional design cannot eliminate these dilemmas; the problems of democratic governance become even more difficult at the international level.

Conclusion

It is unlikely that in the next three decades major wars like those of the twentieth century will alter the balance of power in the international system. Even here we must be careful not to overstate the case for radical changes as a result of the great conflicts of the past century. In 1914 there were eight great powers. In 2001 the number of the largest wealthy economies is seven, the G7, with Russia in attendance to form the G8. The difference? In 1914 Austria-Hungary, Britain, France, Germany, Italy, Japan, Russia and the United States were the Great Powers, and in 2001 the G8 comprises Britain, Canada, France, Germany, Italy, Japan and the United States, plus Russia. Canada has replaced the defunct Austria-Hungary. The United States is far more powerful both economically and militarily than Britain was as the declining hegemon of the international order in 1914. This is not complacent; wealth and power do tend to reproduce themselves. It also does not mean, as chapter 3 indicates, that there will not be wars or that the Great Powers will enjoy untroubled peace, but the enemies they will face will be diverse, most of them not states, rather than each other.

The big three economic powers – the EU, the USA and Japan – are likely to dominate the world economy well into the next century. Indeed, the G7 countries are unlikely to be overtaken as the great powers, whether economic or military. None of the possible contenders – Brazil, China, India or Russia – are likely to attain that level of GDP per capita that is essential to being a major player in the world economy at the same time as being able to sustain a large military expenditure without an excessive burden on the civilian population. The world will remain grossly unequal and success in economic modernization is likely to be confined to a minority of the developing countries.

This continuing combination of wealth and poverty will prove explosive because the institutions of international governance are supposed to be inclusive. Increasing pressure will be put on international institutions to change policies to focus on the needs of the developing world in a way that does more than reflect the outlook of the OECD. This will lead to conflict within and pressure on bodies like the IMF and the WTO. The wealthy countries will, however, continue to pay for and thus control these institutions, but they may be forced to become more cautious, seeking greater legitimacy for their decisions. International governance through the G7 and the institutions it controls may just contain the effects of the conventional economic turbulence. Meltdown in international financial markets will probably continue to be prevented, but at the cost of expensive rescues of bankers and foreign investors. This will not enable the system to pursue ambitious goals like tackling world poverty or preventing environmental degradation. The pessimistic conclusion may thus be that there will be enough governance to keep the system intact until it faces problems that are beyond governance.

Some states will thus matter for the foreseeable future both in domestic economic policy and as the key props of the institutions of international governance. The belief that state sovereignty is being undermined rests on an overestimation of the economic governance capacities of states in the recent past and the belief that the internal affairs of states were far more inviolate in the past than they are today. States have never been 'sovereign' in the sense of having the capacity to be stand-alone governors of every aspect of their societies. Given sufficient wealth and competence, they will continue to be the key actors in domestic social and economic policy and the primary actors in external economic and political policy. The sort of 'sovereignty' claimed by Slobodan Milosovic, the equivalent of the right in Roman law to use and abuse one's property as one willed, has never been conceded in practice by the other states in the international system. States have never been able to behave beyond toleration, whether internally or externally, although action and intervention have depended on policy and prudence. Intervention in the past often took the form of imperialism or colonialism. Sometimes, however, it gave sanction to norms. Moreover, we should be cautious and not imagine that an active policy of intervention to protect 'human rights', in countries too poor, too weak or too illegitimate to object effectively will look so different from the fumbling and cynical efforts of the powers in the nineteenth century and early twentieth century.

A world living on the legacy in the international system of the embedded liberalism created after 1945 and still dominated by the Great Powers, led by the United States, acting in concert with and through the international institutions that they fund, is still the most likely outcome for the international system in the early part of this century. Thereafter, the problems of environmental crisis, population growth and world poverty will make this system increasingly hard to sustain. In the medium term these problems will not create forces capable of shaking Western hegemony, but they will be capable of making its rule ever more difficult and less legitimate. It is almost impossible to see the present world order as sustainable in the long run, it is so unfair and environmentally destructive. The populations of the advanced countries, especially the USA, will not be willing to reduce oil and energy consumption until faced with probably irreversible effects. They are equally unlikely to accept more generous resource transfers to the poorest or support for migrants and refugees. The problem now is that the system lacks credible gravediggers: there are forces capable of disturbing the peace of the rich, but not of replacing them.

Notes

1 Military Revolutions

1 This is not an attempt to resurrect 'technological determinism', although it gives a leading role to technology in driving social change in methods of warfare. The real problem with such determinism is not technology *per se*, but the privileging of a particular factor into a scheme of general social causality. It is also necessary to recognize that within any particular 'technology' there are always options, paths taken and untaken, and that these paths are often disrupted and changed by subsequent developments. Technology is neither the unfolding of an evolutionary potential inherent in it, nor is it always constrained to develop in a path-dependent manner set by an early lock-in. The technologies discussed here were variants from a range of possibilities; thus there were alternative designs to the bastioned trace fortress, and rifles and breech-loading guns were available in the sixteenth century. See C. Sabel and J. Zeitlin, 'Introduction', in Sabel and Zeitlin (eds), *World of Possibilities* (Cambridge: Cambridge University Press 1998).

2 Michael Roberts, *The Military Revolution 1560–1660* (inaugural lecture) (Belfast: Belfast University Press, 1956), reprinted in his *Essays in Swedish History* (London: Weidenfeld and Nicolson, 1967) and in C. J. Rogers (ed.), *The Military Revolution Debate: Readings on the Military Transfor-*

mation of Early Modern Europe (Boulder: Westview, 1995). The latter is a useful collection which includes several other major essays on the topic.

3 Cited in B. S. Hall, *Weapons and Warfare in Renaissance Europe* (Baltimore: Johns Hopkins University Press, 1997) p. 159. This is the best discussion of the technology and tactics of the gunpowder revolution.

4 On the Ottomans see R. Murphey, *Ottoman Warfare 1500–1700* (London: UCL Press, 1999) and V. Askan, 'Ottoman war and warfare 1453–1812', in J. Black (ed.) *War in the Early Modern World 1450–1815* (London: UCL Press, 1999). On Spain see G. Parker, *The Army of Flanders and the Spanish Road 1567–1659* (Cambridge: Cambridge University Press, 1972). One should remember that forms of warfare sometimes do strongly favour the offensive. For example, Western Europe had no effective answer to the Mongol invasions of the thirteenth century. These were based on the combination of fast-moving steppe cavalry and Chinese siege warfare. Only the intrinsic weakness of the Mongol tribal confederation as a political system saved much of Europe from conquest.

5 See W. McNeill, *Keeping Together in Time: Dance and Drill in Human History* (Cambridge: Harvard University Press, 1995), ch. 5.

6 T. F. Arnold 'Fortifications and the military revolution: the Gonzaga experience 1530–1630', in Rogers, *The Military Revolution Debate*.

7 Edward Gibbon, *The Decline and Fall of the Roman Empire*, abridged D. M. Low (London: Chatto and Windus, 1960), pp. 528–9.

8 Guibert, *Essai general de tactique*, quoted in G. Best, *War and Society in Revolutionary Europe 1770–1870* (London: Fontana, 1982), p. 58. See also for Guibert, R. R. Palmer 'Frederick the Great, Guibert, Bulow: from dynastic to national war', in P. Paret (ed.), *Makers of Modern Strategy* (Oxford: Clarendon, 1986).

9 See Carl von Clausewitz, *On War*, trans. M. Howard and P. Paret (Princeton: Princeton University Press, 1989) and P.

Paret, *Clausewitz and the State* (Princeton: Princeton University Press, 1985).

10 Bloch cited in J. F. C. Fuller, *The Conduct of War* (London: Methuen, 1979) p. 130.

11 G. Hardach, *The First World War 1914–18*, vol. 2 of *History of the World Economy in the Twentieth Century* (London: Allen Lane, 1977), p. 6, table 3.

12 Ibid., p. 5, table 1.

13 Ibid., p. 148, table 18.

14 Ibid., p. 290. See also A. Milward, *War, Economy and Society*, vol. 5 of *History of the World Economy in the Twentieth Century* (London: Allen Lane, 1977) for an account of economic management in the Second World War.

15 See B. Bond and M. Alexander, 'Liddell Hart and De Gaulle: the doctrines of limited liability and mobile defence', and D. MacIsaac, 'Voices from the central blue: the air power theorists', both in Paret, *Makers of Modern Strategy*.

16 B. Brodie, *The Absolute Weapon* (1946), cited by L. Freedman, *The Evolution of Nuclear Strategy* (London: Macmillan, 1981), p. 44.

2 The International System in the Westphalian Era

1 On territorial exclusiveness see J. G. Ruggie, 'Territoriality and beyond: problematising modernity in international relations', *International Organisation* 47, no. 1 (1993) pp. 134–72, and on the evolution of sovereignty S. D. Krasner, 'Sovereignty: an institutional perspective', *Comparative Political Studies* 21, no. 1 (1988), pp. 66–94.

2 See J. Strayer, *On the Medieval Origins of the Modern State* (Princeton: Princeton University Press, 1970).

3 J. Bodin, *On Sovereignty* (1576), ed. J. H. Franklin (Cambridge: Cambridge University Press, 1992).

4 See A. MacKay, *Spain in the Middles Ages: From Frontier to Empire 1000–1500* (Basingstoke: Macmillan, 1977), repr. 1993), p. 105.

5   See M. Mann, *The Sources of Social Power*, vol. 1: *A History of Power from the Beginning to AD 1760* (Cambridge: Cambridge University Press, 1986), pp. 453–55. See also M. van Creveld, *The Rise and Decline of the State* (Cambridge: Cambridge University Press, 1999), pp. 156–60, B. D. Porter, *War and the Rise of the State* (New York: Free Press, 1994), and B. M. Downing, *The Military Revolution and Political Change: Origins of Democracy and Autocracy in Early Modern Europe* (Princeton: Princeton University Press, 1992).

6   See Downing, *The Military Revolution and Political Change*.

7   On the weakness of the concept of absolutist regimes see M. Henshall, *The Myth of Absolutism* (London: Longman, 1992). The most satisfactory account of differences in types of early modern regime is T. Ertman, *Birth of the Leviathan* (Cambridge: Cambridge University Press, 1997).

8   H. Spruyt, *The Sovereign State and its Competitors* (Princeton: Princeton University Press, 1994).

9   See P. Dollinger, *The German Hansa* (London: Macmillan, 1964).

10 See A. Pichierri, *Città Stato: Economia e politica del modello anseatico* (Venice: Marsilio, 1997).

11 See Spruyt, *The Sovereign State and its Competitors*.

12 See A. Giddens, *A Contemporary Critique of Historical Materialism*, vol. 2: *The Nation-State and Violence* (Cambridge: Polity, 1985).

13 See S. D. Krasner, 'Westphalia and all that', in J. Goldstein and R. O. Keohane (eds), *Ideas and Foreign Policy: Beliefs, Institutions and Political Change* (Ithaca: Cornell University Press, 1993) and S. D. Krasner 'Compromising Westphalia', *International Security* 20, no. 3 (Winter 1995–6), pp. 115–51.

14 C. Schmitt, *The Concept of the Political* (New Brunswick: Rutgers University Press, 1976); C. Schmitt, *Political Theology: Four Chapters on the Concept of Sovereignty* (Cambridge: MIT Press, 1985); and R. Koselleck, *Critique and Crisis: Enlightenment and the Pathogenesis of Modern Society* (Oxford: Berg, 1988).

15 R. O. Keohane (ed.), *Neo-realism and its Critics* (New York: Columbia University Press, 1986).

16 See S. Bromley, 'The logic of liberal sovereignty', MS, Open University, 1999.

17 On this aspect of the formation of market liberalism see Karl Polanyi, *The Great Transformation* (1944) (Boston: Beacon Press, 1957).

18 Immanuel Kant, *Perpetual Peace* (1795), in *Kant's Political Writings*, ed. H. S. Reiss (Cambridge: Cambridge University Press, 1977), and W. B. Gallie, *Philosophers of Peace and War* (Cambridge: Cambridge University Press, 1978).

19 B. Eichengreen, *Globalizing Capital: A History of the International Monetary System* (Princeton: Princeton University Press, 1996), ch. 2 on the Gold Standard.

20 P. Hirst and G. Thompson, *Globalization in Question*, 2nd edn (Cambridge: Polity, 1999), p. 27, table 2.3.

21 P. Hirst and G. Thompson, 'Globalization in one country', *Economy and Society* 29, no. 3 (2000) p. 30, table 4.

22 Cobden cited in B. Semmel, *Liberalism and Naval Strategy: Ideology, Interest and Sea Power during the Pax Britannica* (Boston: Allen and Unwin, 1986), p. 71.

23 See J. E. Thomson, *Mercenaries, Pirates and Sovereigns: State-Building and Extraterritorial Violence in Early Modern Europe* (Princeton: Princeton University Press, 1994).

24 See M. Mazower, *Dark Continent* (London: Penguin 1999).

25 See J. G. Ruggie, *Constructing the World Polity* (London: Routledge, 1998), ch. 2: 'Embedded liberalism and the postwar economic regimes'.

3 The Future of War

1 For GDP figures see World Bank, *World Development Report 1999–2000* (New York: Oxford University Press, 1999). On the size of Russia's economy and why it tends to be overestimated see C. Gaddy and B. Ickes, 'Beyond the bailout: time to face reality about Russia's "virtual economy" ', *Foreign Affairs* (Sept.–Oct. 1998), pp. 53–67.

2 See J. S. Nye and W. A. Owens, 'America's information edge', *Foreign Affairs* (Mar.–Apr. 1996) pp. 20–36.

3 See M. Ignatieff, *Virtual War – Kosovo and Beyond* (London: Chatto and Windus, 2000) and M. Kaldor, *New and Old Wars: Organized Violence in the Global Era* (Cambridge: Polity, 1999). For a criticism of such leftist advocacy of military intervention from the left see Noam Chomsky, *The New Military Humanism: Lessons from Kosovo* (London: Pluto, 1999).

4 Kaldor, *New and Old Wars*, p. 148.

5 See E. A. Cohen, 'A revolution in warfare', *Foreign Affairs* (Mar.–Apr. 1996), pp. 37–54.

6 M. Libicki, 'The small and the many', in J. Arquilla and D. Ronfeldt (eds), *In Athena's Camp: Preparing for Conflict in the Information Age* (Santa Monica: RAND, 1997).

7 M. O'Hanlon, *Technological Change and the Future of Warfare* (Washington: Brookings Institution Press, 2000).

8 A. Nicoll, 'Let slip the drones of war', *Financial Times*, 14 Aug. 2000, p. 17; 'Moving targets of warfare', *Financial Times*, 4 Jan. 2000; D. Hambling, 'I spy with my little fly', *Guardian*, 21 Oct. 1999, p. S2.

9 E. N. Luttwak, 'A post-heroic military policy', *Foreign Affairs* (July–Aug. 1996) pp. 33–44.

10 R. J. Newman, 'The new space race', *US News and World Report*, 8 Nov. 1999, pp. 30–8.

11 See D. Kahn, *The Codebreakers*, rev. edn (New York: Simon and Schuster, 1997) and R. V. Jones, *Most Secret War: British Scientific Intelligence 1939–1945* (London: Hamish Hamilton, 1978).

12 B. D. Berkowitz, 'Warfare in the information age', in Arquilla and Ronfeldt, *In Athena's Camp*.

13 On the prospects for chemical and biological warfare see J. B. Alexander, *Future War* (New York: St Martin's Press, 1999), chs 6 and 11. This deals with non-lethal weapons – I have ignored them here since the military will always prefer weapons that kill except in exceptional situations like crowd control.

14 M. Mandelbaum, 'Is major war obsolete?', *Survival* 4, no. 4

(Winter 1998–9) pp. 20–38, and J. Mueller, *Retreat from Doomsday: The Obsolescence of Modern War* (New York: Basic Books, 1989).

15 On the future of military organization see C. Moskos et al. (eds), *The Postmodern Military: Armed Forces after the Cold War* (New York and Oxford: Oxford University Press, 2000).

16 A. Toffler and H. Toffler, *War and Anti-War* (Boston: Little Brown, 1993).

17 S. Huntington, *The Clash of Civilizations and the Remaking of World Order* (New York: Simon and Schuster, 1996).

18 The classic modern statement of the proposition that liberal democracies do not fight one another is M. Doyle, 'Kant, liberal legacies and foreign affairs', *Philosophy and Public Affairs* 12, no. 3 (Summer 1983) and 'Liberalism and world politics', *American Political Science Review* 80, no. 4 (1986).

19 The Intergovernmental Panel on Climate Change, sponsored by the UN, produced a draft report in 2000 that revised its estimates of global warming dramatically upwards since its 1995 report. It now presents a worst-case scenario of average global temperatures 6°C above the 1990 level by 2100. Average temperatures today are 5°C higher than those at the end of the last ice age. See J. Vidal, 'Earth will get hotter than expected', *Guardian*, 27 Oct. 2000, p. 18, and V. Houlder and C. Cookson, 'A world of difference', *Financial Times* 4 Nov. 2000, p. 17. The UK's Hadley Centre for Climate Prediction warns of temperatures not equalled since the era of the Dinosaurs, T. Radford, 'Climate – scientists warn new forests would make effects worse', *Guardian*, 9 Nov. 2000, p. 10. On the science of climate change see J. Houghton, *Global Warming: The Complete Briefing* (Cambridge: Cambridge University Press, 1997) and F. Drake, *Global Warming: The Science of Climate Change* (London: Arnold, 2000).

20 States do fight over resources, for example, lack of oil was a major reason for Japan's attack on the US in 1941. Asia is still woefully short of oil and this could lead to conflict, see K. E. Calder, 'Asia's empty gas tank', *Foreign Affairs*

(Mar.–Apr. 1996), pp. 55–69. On population growth see M. Tobias, *World War III: Population and the Biosphere at the End of the Millennium* (New York: Continuum, 1998).

21 See the debate in *Foreign Affairs* (Mar.–Apr. 1996): R. Bernstein and R. H. Munro, 'China: the coming conflict with America', pp. 18–32 and R. S. Ross, 'Beijing as a conservative power', pp. 33–44.

22 On the real state of the Chinese economy and China's multiple social problems see J. Becker, *The Chinese* (London: John Murray, 2000).

4   The Future of the International System

1 See, for example, S. Strange, *The Retreat of the State* (Cambridge: Cambridge University Press, 1996) and S. Sassen, *Losing Control – Sovereignty in an Age of Globalization* (New York: Columbia University Press, 1998).

2 K. Ohmae, *The Borderless World* (London: Collins, 1990); K. Ohmae, *The End of the Nation State* (London: Harper Collins, 1995); D. Korten, *When Corporations Rule the World* (London: Earthscan, 1996).

3 A. Minc, *Le Nouveau Moyen Age* (Paris: Gallimard, 1993); P. Cerny, 'Neomedievalism, civil war and the new security dilemma: globalization as durable disorder', *Civil Wars* 1, no .1 (1999), pp. 36–64.

4 M. Castells, *The Information Age*, vol. 2: *The Power of Identity* (Oxford: Blackwell, 1997), p. 359.

5 D. Held, *Democracy and the Global Order: From the Modern State to Cosmopolitan Governance* (Cambridge: Polity, 1995).

6 For a fuller account see P. Hirst and G. Thompson, *Globalization in Question*, 2nd edn (Cambridge: Polity, 1999) – all data cited below are from this source unless separately noted.

7 P. Doremus et al., *The Myth of the Global Corporation* (Princeton: Princeton University Press, 1998); see also W. Ruigrok and R. van Tulder, *The Logic of Global Restructuring* (London: Routledge, 1995).

8   A. Rugman, *The End of Globalization* (London: Random House Business Books, 2000).

9   G. Thompson, 'Are there any limits to "globalization"? International trade, capital flows and borders', contact g.f.thompson@open.ac.uk and J. F. Helliwell, *How Much do National Borders Matter?* (Washington DC: Brookings Institution, 1998).

10 Rugman, *The End of Globalization*, p. 8, table 1.2.

11 United Nations Development Programme, *Human Development Report 1999* (Oxford and New York: Oxford University Press, 1999), p. 62.

12 For boosterish accounts of the New Economy see D. Coyle *The Weightless World* (Oxford: Capstone, 1997) and C. Leadbeater, *Living on Thin Air – the New Economy* (London: Viking, 1999). For a sober assessment of digital markets see J. B. De Long and A. M. Froomkin, 'Speculative microeconomics for tomorrow's economy', contact delong@econ.berkeley.edu; on dotcoms and intellectual property, C. May, 'Reifying markets, misreading decline: the continuing salience of states in the information age'; contact christopher.may@uwe.ac.uk; and on dotcom democracy, T. Tranvik, 'Global dotcom democracy', Norwegian Centre for Research in Organisation and Management, Bergen University, 2000.

13 D. Gordon, *Fat and Mean: The Corporate Squeeze of Working Americans and the Myth of Managerial Downsizing* (New York: Free Press, 1996).

14 See Hirst and Thompson, *Globalization in Question*, ch. 5: 'Can the welfare state survive globalization?'

15 E. H. Carr, *The Twenty Years' Crisis 1919–1939* (London: Macmillan, 1939).

16 J. Weiner, *Globalisation and the Harmonisation of Law* (London: Pinter, 1999).

17 This point is well made by R. M. Unger, 'The really new Bretton Woods', in M. Uzan (ed.), *The Financial System under Stress: An Architecture for a New World Economy* (London: Routledge, 1996).

18 See the outline by D. Held and the critique by M. Saward

in B. Holden (ed.), *Global Democracy, Key Debates* (London: Routledge, 2000).

19 UNDP, *Human Development Report 1999*, p. 2.

20 On the possibility of democratic accountability of international organization there is a useful debate with contributions by D. Held, R. A. Dahl and J. Tobin in I. Shapiro and C. Hacker-Córdon, *Democracy's Edges* (Cambridge: Cambridge University Press, 1999).

Further Reading

1 Military Revolutions

M. S. Anderson, *War and Society in Europe of the Old Regime 1618–1789*. London: Fontana, 1988.

G. Best, *War and Society in Revolutionary Europe 1770–1870*. London: Fontana, 1982.

J. Black, *War and the World: Military Power and the Fate of Continents 1450–2000*. New Haven: Yale University Press, 1998.

B. Bond, *War and Society in Europe 1870–1970*. London: Fontana, 1984.

J. Brewer, *The Sinews of Power: War, Money and the English State 1688–1783*. London: Routledge, 1989.

L. Freedman, *The Evolution of Nuclear Strategy*. London: Macmillan, 1981.

J. Glete, *Warfare at Sea: Maritime Conflicts and the Transformation of Europe*. London: Routledge, 2000.

J. R. Hale, *War and Society in Renaissance Europe 1450–1620*. London: Fontana, 1985.

D. Hounshell, *From the American System to Mass Production 1800–1932*. Baltimore: Johns Hopkins University Press, 1984.

W. MacNeill, *The Pursuit of Power: Technology, Armed Force and Society since AD 1000*. Oxford: Blackwell, 1983.

P. Paret (ed.), *Makers of Modern Strategy from Machiavelli to the Nuclear Age*. Oxford: Clarendon, 1986.

G. Parker, *The Military Revolution: Military Innovation and the

Rise of the West 1500–1800, 2nd edn. Cambridge: Cambridge University Press, 1998.

M. Pearton, *The Knowledgeable State: Diplomacy, War and Technology since 1830.* London: Burnett Books/Hutchinson, 1982.

H. Strachan, *European Armies and the Conduct of War.* London: Routledge, 2000.

F. Tallett, *War and Society in Early Modern Europe 1495–1715.* London: Routledge, 1992.

M. van Creveld, *Supplying War: Logistics from Wallenstein to Patton.* Cambridge: Cambridge University Press, 1977.

2   The International System in the Westphalian Era

P. B. Evans et al. (eds), *Bringing the State Back In,* Cambridge: Cambridge University Press, 1985.

F. H. Hinsley, *Power and the Pursuit of Peace.* Cambridge: Cambridge University Press, 1967.

F. H. Hinsley, *Sovereignty,* 2nd edn. Cambridge: Cambridge University Press, 1986.

E. J. Hobsbawm, *The Age of Extremes: The Short Twentieth Century 1914–1991.* London: Michael Joseph, 1994.

P. Kennedy, *The Rise and Fall of the Great Powers: Economic Change and Military Conflict from 1500 to 2000.* London: Fontana, 1989.

S. D. Krasner, *Sovereignty.* Princeton: Princeton University Press, 1999.

R. MacKenney, *The City State 1500–1700: Republican Liberty in an Age of Princely Power.* Atlantic Highlands: Humanities Press International, 1989.

M. Mazower, *Dark Continent,* London: Penguin, 1999.

G. Parker, *The Thirty Years' War.* London: Routledge and Kegan Paul, 1987.

T. K. Rabb, *The Struggle for Political Stability in Europe.* New York: Oxford University Press, 1975.

J. G. Ruggie, *Building the World Polity: Essays on International Institutionalisation.* London: Routledge, 1998.

J. H. Shennan, *The Origins of the European State*. London: Hutchinson, 1974.

H. Spruyt, *The Sovereign State and its Competitors*. Princeton: Princeton University Press, 1994.

W. Te Brake, *Shaping History: Ordinary People in European Politics 1500–1700*. Berkeley: University of California Press, 1998.

C. Tilly, *Coercion, Capital and European States AD 990–1990*. Oxford: Blackwell, 1990.

M. van Creveld, *The Rise and Decline of the State*. Cambridge: Cambridge University Press, 1999.

3   The Future of War

J. Arquilla and D. Ronfeldt (eds), *In Athena's Camp: Preparing for Conflict in the Information Age*. Santa Monica: RAND, 1997.

J. Black, *War: Past, Present and Future*. Stroud: Sutton, 2000.

V. Bornschier and C. Chase-Dunn (eds), *The Future of Global Conflict*. London: Sage, 1999.

A. H. Cordesman and A. R. Wagner, *The Lessons of Modern War*, vol. 1: *The Arab–Israeli Conflicts 1973–89*; vol. 2: *The Iran–Iraq War*; vol. 3: *The Afghan and Falklands Conflicts*. Boulder: Westview Press, 1990.

M. De Landa, *War in the Age of Intelligent Machines*. New York: Swerve, 1991.

L. Freedman, *The Revolution in Strategic Affairs*, Adelphi Paper 318, International Institute for Strategic Studies. Oxford: Oxford University Press, 1998.

L. Freedman and E. Karsh, *The Gulf Conflict 1990–91*. London: Faber, 1993.

F. Heisbourg, *The Future of Warfare*. London: Orion. 1997.

M. Ignatieff, *The Warrior's Honour: Ethnic War and the Modern Conscience*. London: Chatto and Windus, 1998.

M. Ignatieff, *Virtual War: Kosovo and Beyond*. London: Chatto and Windus, 2000.

International Institute for Strategic Studies, 'The future of strategy and war', special issue, *Survival* vol. 40, no. 4 (Winter 1998–9).

M. Kaldor, *New and Old Wars: Organized Violence in a Global Era*. Cambridge: Polity Press, 1999.

M. O'Hanlon, *Technological Change and the Future of War*. Washington DC: Brookings Institution Press, 2000.

A. Toffler and H. Toffler, *War and Anti-War: Survival at the Dawn of the Twenty-First Century*. Boston: Little Brown, 1993.

M. van Creveld, *On Future War*. London: Brassey's, 1991.

4 The Future of the International System

M. Castells, *The Information Age: Economy, Society and Culture*, vol. 1: *The Rise of the Network Society* (1996); vol. 2: *The Power of Identity* (1997); vol. 3: *The End of the Millennium* (1997). Oxford: Blackwell.

B. Eichengreen, *Towards a New International Financial Architecture*. Washington DC: Institute for International Economics, 1999.

R. Gilpin, *The Challenge of Global Capitalism: The World Economy in the Twenty-First Century*. Princeton: Princeton University Press, 2000.

J. Gray, *False Dawn: The Delusions of Global Capitalism*. London: Granta, 1998.

F. Halliday, *The World at 2000*. Basingstoke: Palgrave, 2001.

R. Heilbronner, *Twenty-First Century Capitalism*. London: UCL Press, 1995.

D. Held and A. McGrew, D. Goldblatt and J. Perraton, *Global Transformations*. Cambridge: Polity, 1999.

A. Hurrell and N. Woods (eds), *Inequality, Globalization and World Politics*. Oxford: Oxford University Press, 1999.

P. Kennedy, *Preparing for the Twenty-First Century*. New York: Random House, 1993.

P. B. Kennen, *Managing the World Economy: Fifty Years after Bretton Woods*. Washington DC: Institute for International Economics, 1994.

D. Rodrik, *Has Globalization Gone Too Far?* Washington DC: Institute for International Economics, 1997.

J. Rosenau and E. O. Czempiel (eds), *Governance without Government*. Cambridge: Cambridge University Press, 1992.

G. Soros, *The Crisis of Global Capitalism*. London: Little Brown, 1998.

L. Weiss, *The Myth of the Powerless State*. Cambridge: Polity, 1998.

Index

Ignatieff, Michael 82
industrialization and war 24, 26–9
information war 93–4
International Monetary Fund (IMF) 75, 118, 133, 136, 139, 145
international norms 57, 69–71
International system
  evolution in twenty-first century 110–11, 130–1, 135–6, 145–6
  formation 76–8
  reconstruction 1944–5
internet 122–3

Kaldor, Mary 82–3, 86–8
Kant, Immanuel 64–5
Keynesianism 74
Knox, John 52
Korten, David 113
Koselleck, Reinhard 58
Kosovo 41, 82, 85–7, 91, 94, 96
Kyoto accords 140

levée en masse/conscription 21
liberalism 61–4
liberal international economy 64–6, 71, 73–6
liberal internationalism 64–5
liberal democracies and war 101–2
Libicki, Martin 89–90
Long Term Capital Management 118
Lübeck 51,55

Mao Tse Tung 38
Marx, Karl 76
mechanized war 33–5
medieval state, characteristics 45–7
Metternich, Prince 62
military intellectuals 9, 20, 25, 29–30, 36
military revolutions
  general 1, 7–9, 40–1
  sixteenth and seventeenth century 7, 10–14, 17–18, 48
Milosevic, Slobodan 84–6, 147
Minc, Alain 113
Mongols 150n4
Multilateral Agreement on Investment (MAI) 138–9
mutual recognition of states 56

Napoleonic warfare 21–2
national economies/ mercantilism 60–1
nationalism 60–2
network Society 113
New Economy 111–12, 122–4
New Middle Ages 113, 129–30
'new wars' 82–8
non-governmental organizations (NGOs) 111, 114, 133, 138

305727330U